HANDS & FEET

Audio Adrenaline

HANDS & FEET

Audio Adrenaline

Regal

From Gospel Light
Ventura, California, U.S.A.

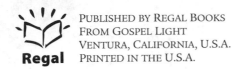

PUBLISHED BY REGAL BOOKS
FROM GOSPEL LIGHT
VENTURA, CALIFORNIA, U.S.A.
PRINTED IN THE U.S.A.

Regal Books is a ministry of Gospel Light, a Christian publisher dedicated to serving the local church. We believe God's vision for Gospel Light is to provide church leaders with biblical, user-friendly materials that will help them evangelize, disciple and minister to children, youth and families.

It is our prayer that this Regal book will help you discover biblical truth for your own life and help you meet the needs of others. May God richly bless you.

For a free catalog of resources from Regal Books/Gospel Light, please call your Christian supplier or contact us at 1-800-4-GOSPEL or www.regalbooks.com.

Cover design by Josh Talbot Design (www.joshuatalbotdesign.com). Photos by Karen Bosch, Rebekah DeFord, Patti Johnson, Chris Kempel, Marcia Kilgallen and Mike Trozzo.

Library of Congress Cataloging-in-Publication Data
The Hands and Feet Project / Audio Adrenaline
    p. cm.
  ISBN 0-8307-3932-7 (trade paper)
  1. Hands and Feet Project. 2. Missions—Haiti. 3. Orphanages—Haiti. 4. Haiti—Church history. 5. Audio Adrenaline (Musical group) I. Audio Adrenaline (Musical group)

BV2848.H3H36 2006
266.0097294'086945—dc22   2006019313

1   2   3   4   5   6   7   8   9   10   /   10   /   09   08   07   06

Rights for publishing this book in other languages are contracted by Gospel Light Worldwide, the international nonprofit ministry of Gospel Light. Gospel Light Worldwide also provides publishing and technical assistance to international publishers dedicated to producing Sunday School and Vacation Bible School curricula and books in the languages of the world. For additional information, visit www.gospellightworldwide.org; write to Gospel Light Worldwide, P.O. Box 3875, Ventura, CA 93006; or send an e-mail to info@gospellightworldwide.org.

Contents

HANDS & FEET

Audio Adrenaline

An image flashed across my TV screen
Another broken heart comes into view
I saw the pain and I turned my back
Why can't I do the things I want to?
I'm willing yet I'm so afraid
You give me strength
When I say . . .

I want to be Your hands
I want to be Your feet
I'll go where You send me
I'll go where You send me

And I try, yeah, I try
To touch the world like You touched my life
And I'll find my way
To be Your hands

I've abandoned every selfish thought
I've surrendered every thing I've got
You can have everything I am
And perfect everything I'm not
I'm willing, I'm not afraid
You give me strength when I say . . .

I want to be Your hands
I want to be Your feet
I'll go where You send me
I'll go where You send me

This is the last time
I turn my back on You
From now on, I'll go out
Send me where You want me to
I finally have a mission
I promise I'll complete
I don't need excuses
When I am Your hands and feet . . .

THE JOURNEY

A tropical day. A beautiful beach. Children playing on the water's edge. A seemingly idyllic place. But this is Haiti. Although it is a place of amazing beauty and friendly people, it is also one of the poorest countries on our planet. It is a country plagued with hunger, disease and political strife. It is a country in which every night millions of children go to bed with empty stomachs. It is a country in which millions are enslaved by the falsehoods of voodoo.

It is one of my favorite countries in the world.

Many years ago, before we started Audio Adrenaline, my parents served as missionaries in Haiti. I was lucky enough to get to visit on my summer vacations. It was then that God gave me a heart for Haiti and for its beautiful people, especially the children.

Soon afterward, I embarked on my crazy career with Audio Adrenaline. God has so blessed Audio A over the years, and one of our responses to those blessings has been to start The Hands and Feet Project in Cyvadier, Haiti.

We started the project to provide a place for orphaned children in Haiti to have a roof over their heads and plenty of food to eat, as well as to come to a saving knowledge of Jesus Christ as their savior. It's also a place where people from the States can come and see what it is like to serve and to be the hands and feet of Jesus to the people of Haiti.

This book tells the story of The Hands and Feet Project. I hope you enjoy it and that you too come to a better understanding of what joy it is to serve Christ through serving others.

God bless,

Mark Stuart

Chapter 1
FLIGHT TO HAITI

For so long I've been sleeping
Dead inside
In so many ways, so many ways I've tried to hide
You breathed deep into me Your melody

"MELODY [LOST INSIDE THE WONDER]"
AUDIO ADRENALINE

Mark Stuart and Will McGinnis, two members of the veteran rock band Audio Adrenaline, stand in line at a Starbucks coffee counter in the Miami, Florida, airport, waiting for their flight to Haiti to be announced. People hurry past them, moving swiftly from one gate to another, rushing to one of many airport lines, bags slung over shoulders and suitcases dragging along behind.

Standing with Mark and Will is Chris Cotton, a lawyer who recently moved back to Nashville, Tennessee, from California to work with Audio Adrenaline and others on a venture called The Hands and Feet Project. He and Will are deep in conversation about the state of the Church today. In between thoughts, Chris manages to reach the front of the line and order. "I'd just like a Grande drip, please. Thanks."

Once Chris has received his morning beverage, he steps over to the condiment area. Moments later he is joined again by Will, who returns to their conversation. "Unity," Mark says. "That's what I think the Church is lacking today. Unity. If we can't live in unity with one another as believers, how can we ever show a watching world what God's love and acceptance is all about? Do you know what I mean?" Chris nods.

With all the determination and care of a master craftsman, Will adds just the right amount of additives to perfect his caffeinated masterpiece. He closes his eyes and slowly savors the first sip. "Ahh," he says. "Sweet nectar of the gods."

A loudspeaker crackles on, booming the voice of the flight attendant through the halls of the airport: *This is American Flight 803 with non-stop service to Port-au-Prince. Soon we will begin the boarding process. We will begin boarding by group number and at this time we'd like to invite our passengers to begin lining up . . .*

With Starbucks coffee cups in hand, Mark, Will and Chris move over to where Drex and Jo Stuart, Mark's parents, are waiting in line to board the plane. Each person on the team knows full well that in less than two hours, they will be in the island nation of Haiti. The trip is a jolt, especially for those who've never been to the small country before. In a short amount of time, travelers move from the wealthy American world populated by coffee shops on every corner to a Third World country overflowing with enormous needs.

The team had left that morning from Nashville, Tennessee, not too far from Franklin, Tennessee, the place Mark and Will call home. It was an early Friday morning flight scheduled to take off well before dawn, so the group was in need of their morning caffeination. Mark and Will look especially exhausted. Audio Adrenaline has been touring hard the past month, and only days before, Mark and Will had finished up a tough road schedule with a couple shows in Anchorage, Alaska. They arrived home late on Wednesday night. Now, only two short days later, they were again boarding a plane to another destination. This time, however, they would be traveling to a much different venue: the site of The Hands and Feet Project.

This is American Flight 803, with non-stop service to Port-au-Prince. Soon we will begin the boarding process. At this time, we'd like to invite group one to board . . .

The story of how Audio Adrenaline began goes a little something like this: One day back in the 1980s, Mark Stuart and fellow classmate Barry Blair were on the campus of Kentucky Christian College in Grayson, Kentucky, and began talking about the possibilities of starting a band. Will McGinnis and his mother happened to be on campus that same day, and while she was taking a walk around, she overheard Mark and Barry chatting. She approached Mark and Barry and said that her son, Will, played bass and that they should invite him to join their band. However, when Mark and Barry later approached Will and asked him to join, Will admitted that he was still learning how to play bass. "That's okay," Barry replied. "I'll teach you how to play."

Shortly thereafter, Mark, Will and Barry formed a band called A-180, which quickly became a regional sensation. A-180 started playing shows at Kentucky Christian College every weekend, and soon Ron Gibson and David Stuart, Mark's brother, were added to the lineup. After the members graduated, a friend of the group named Bob Herdman suggested that they all form a new

An aerial photo taken during the descent into Port-au-Prince, the capital of Haiti. Most of the people living in the slums of the city survive on less than one U.S. dollar per day.

band called Audio Adrenaline. Bob had written the lyrics for two songs, but he still needed music for his words. Those two songs later would become "My God" and "DC-10."

The band recorded "My God" and was able get it put on a Christian music compilation that was sent to radio stations under the Audio Adrenaline name. When "My God" climbed the charts and reached the number 5 position, Forefront Records took notice and, based on that one song, offered Audio Adrenaline a recording contract. Bob joined the band, replacing David Stuart on keyboards, and in 1992 the group released its first record, the self-titled *Audio Adrenaline*.

Over the years, band members have come and gone. The current lineup includes Mark Stuart on vocals, Will McGinnis on bass, Tyler Burkum on guitar (founding member Barry Blair left the band in 1996), and Ben Cissell on drums. Yet for 15 years, Audio Adrenaline has continued to produce compassionate and powerful songs, making the band one of the most respected industry stalwarts in all of contemporary Christian music. The band has always thrived on playing live shows, and because of this the members have toured aggressively throughout their careers. By bringing solid performances in every venue, they've earned a loyal fan base and have continued to draw crowds, even through their last tour in 2006.

In terms of numbers, Audio A, as the band is sometimes called by its fans, has sold more than 3 million records and has released more than 18 number-one singles. The band has been nominated for 20 Dove Awards—four of which they won—and has won two Grammy Awards as well. In 2005, Audio Adrenaline released its tenth album, *Until My Heart Caves In*, and in 2006, the group signed off with its aptly titled final album, *Adios*.

Good morning. This is Flight 803 with direct service to Port-au-Prince. We are now boarding all passengers . . .

God planted the seeds for The Hands and Feet Project many years before Audio Adrenaline formed as a band. Mark's parents, Drex and Jo, have been coming to Haiti regularly since 1979. In the beginning, Drex took people from their home church in Kentucky on the trips as a way for those people to get involved in something larger than themselves. But it didn't take long before those short-term trips began to have an unintended impact on Drex. With every passing trip, he became more and more drawn to the people he met. After one of their trips, both Drex and Jo had a sense that God was leading them to invest more of themselves into the people of Haiti. They knew that it was time to jump in with both feet and see what God would do if they committed their whole lives. So the day after Mark graduated from high school, Drex and Jo moved to Haiti.

Over the years, Mark has often traveled to the small nation to be a part of what his parents were doing. "I've always had a love for Haiti," he says. "This is like home for me. When I come here, I just melt into who I am supposed to be."

On some levels, Audio Adrenaline's own ministry and power have sprung out of Mark's experiences in Haiti, and many of the band's songs reflect that lyrically. "Haiti was like the seed of Audio Adrenaline," Mark states. "One came out of the other. The lyrics for the song 'Big House,' which is probably our biggest song, were actually lyrics to a song that the kids in Haiti taught us to sing. I was in junior high or high school on the north shore of Haiti working with my parents, and these kids would be singing this song. It was the most popular song here for 20 years.

"One verse of 'Big House' says, *Do you want to go to my father's house, to my father's house, to my father's house? There is joy, joy, joy.* Another verse in the song says, *Come and go with me to my father's house.* So we wrote 'Big House' using those lyrics. It's just a song about the hope of heaven.

"If you're a kid living here, you most likely live in a hut with a mud floor and a tin roof. You've got 10 family members sleeping with you. You might even have to sleep in a chair or something. Then one day, you look down the street and see a house. You think, *I wonder if that's what heaven is like—a big house with everything we need: a room, a bed and all the food we can eat. Someday, I'll go there, to my Father's house.* So that song means a lot to the kids here. I mean, just to have a place to sleep is an amazing thing! I think that's why it was such a big hit here."

Ironically, when the band first recorded the song and listened to it, they wanted to throw it out. "We didn't want to put it on the album," Mark recalls. "We seriously thought the song was stupid. But one day, my dad heard a recording of it and said, 'That's a good song. You have to put it on the record; it'll be the biggest song out there.'"

And it was.

Flight attendants, please prepare for take-off . . .

On Thursday night, the small team had assembled in Mark Stuart's living room in Franklin, Tennessee. Mark's parents had driven in from Kentucky, where they had been for a short break, and had filled up their minivan with empty bins, their own suitcases and some of their other things from home. The team spent the day making runs to Wal-Mart and Home Depot to gather supplies for the trip the next day. Someone had stacked a mountain of canned food in the center of the room, while an equally impressive mountain of toilet paper sat over near the window.

In the valley between the two mountains lay boxes of dried goods, various cooking utensils, microwave popcorn and Drex's favorite: a strange kind of prefabricated pizza in a box—and not just one box of pizza, but dozens. Noticing that the pizzas were becoming a subject of much discussion, Drex looked around the room incredulously. "What?" he said. "You just can't get good pizza over there!"

Meanwhile, Jo got to work packing everything meticulously in the large, durable bins. "My mom is the master packer," Mark said. "She has a system going here. Everything has a place. We just stay out of her way." An hour later, each bin was filled to the top with utensils and smaller boxes of supplies and food. Holes were drilled in each corner of the bin lids and zip ties were inserted through the holes to lock the lids down. After the packing was complete, Mark symbolically traced a line around one hand and one foot on the side of each bin.

Mark's driving passion to do something tangible to help the people of Haiti became a reality in 2004. On a brief trip, the band decided that it was time to stop simply encouraging others to do something to change the world around them and start doing something themselves.

The band decided to build a children's village, where they could not only help save the lives of Haitian orphans but also allow the children the opportunity to have a more abundant life—while also being exposed to the compassionate and transformational love of Jesus. Of course, they knew that the project needed to be led by someone who knew the country, its culture and needs firsthand. Drex and Jo, Mark's parents, were the obvious choice.

The band purchased a parcel of land in August 2004 and began to raise the necessary funds to get the project off the ground. By March 2005, they had poured the foundations for the main building and had dug a well on the property for water. Groups of young people from the United

States on short-term missions trips visited periodically to help finish the wall that would enclose the property and to construct the two floors of the main building that would house Drex and Jo. A group from Bel Air Presbyterian Church in Bel Air, California, helped finish the first floor of the main building in late summer 2005.

With the first floor complete and the second floor's construction well under way (the second floor was completed in early 2006), Mark, Will and Chris were now on their way back to Haiti to see the progress firsthand, help the construction any way that they could, and reconnect with the people in the small town in which the project was based.

One of those people was Thamara, the project's first orphan. After the first year of her life, Thamara had been taken in by her extended family. However, caring for Thamara proved to be just too much for them, so the family approached a woman named Tina Isenhower for help. Tina, who operates a private school in Cyvadier and had been a missionary in Haiti for more than 20 years, put the family in touch with Drex and Jo at The Hands and Feet Project. Thamara became their first orphan, and suddenly, the project had a face and a name. The message, the vision, the need and the hope suddenly became very tangible for everyone involved.

This was going to be a unique trip, as Drex and Jo were officially saying goodbye to their home that they had long kept in Kentucky and were moving many of their belongings down to the project site permanently. They would be coming back for a wedding in the next few months, but after that, they would focus full-time on getting the orphanage up and running. This meant caring for children every day, a goal that Drex and Jo had been working toward for years. The finish line was in sight, but they knew that it would be just the beginning.

This is your captain speaking. We have reached our cruising altitude of 35,000 feet and we will be touching down in Port-au-Prince in approximately one hour . . .

Haiti is a small nation located in the middle of the Caribbean Sea that shares a bit less than half of the island of Hispaniola with the Dominican Republic. The island is positioned between Cuba to the north and west and Puerto Rico to the south and east. Jamaica and the Cayman Islands are also nearby, almost directly to the west. For perspective, the actual landmass of Haiti is just slightly less than the size of the state of Maryland.

Sounds like a cozy group of islands, but the fact is that with a per capita annual income of roughly $400, Haiti is the poorest nation in the Western Hemisphere.[1] Malnutrition, lack of clean drinking water, and inadequate clothing and housing are the norm in the country, not the exception. Houses consist of cinder-block walls and mud floors. Roofs are made of tin or are thatched with palm or other branches. Most extended families live

Drex and Jo Stuart, cofounders
of The Hands and Feet Children's
Village.

under one roof or in a collection of houses huddled together with a communal charcoal grill for cooking. Telephones, televisions and other items that we in America take for granted are all luxuries that elude the average Haitian. Most have never been to a restaurant. Shoes are few and far between. Some kids even share clothes: One child will wear the only pair of shoes the family owns, while the other will wear the only shirt they own. The next day, they will switch articles of clothing.

Children are hit especially hard by the widespread poverty. Of the just over 8.2 million people who live in Haiti, children under the age of 18 make up almost half of the population. There are 1.2 million children under the age of 5, and over half of these children suffer from malnutrition. Only 25 percent of Haitian children have the vaccines they need to survive, making Haiti the country with the lowest vaccination rate in the world. The infant mortality rate in Haiti is 76 of every 1,000 live births, more than twice that of any other country in the Western Hemisphere.[2] More than 462,000 children in Haiti are orphans.[3] Some of these children are sheltered in orphanages and foster homes, but the majority of these children are forced to sleep on the streets with no food, no shelter, no families and no hope.

This is why the members of Audio Adrenaline formed The Hands and Feet Project: to tackle the growing orphan crisis in the country. The Project is currently building a community of homes in which Haitian orphans can live

healthy, happy lives. The organization is dedicated to providing each child with a loving family environment, a viable
Christian witness, immediate attention to medical needs,
and a proper education.

The driving passion of The Hands and Feet Project
comes directly from the admonition of James 1:27—a call to
rescue orphans from their suffering: "Religion that God
our Father accepts as pure and faultless is this: to look after
the widows and orphans in their distress and to keep oneself from being polluted by the world." The band members
know that in the same way that our children here in the
United States are the future of America, Haiti's children
represent the future of Haiti. If there is hope to be found in
this small country, it will only be found in the children who
will grow up one day to run it. So to help these children, one
child at a time, is to help the future leaders of communities,
of cities and of the entire nation. It all begins with the children, who need love, hugs and a caring family to call home.

*In just a few moments, we will begin our final descent into
Port-au-Prince. Please stow your tray tables and bring your seat
forward to its full and upright position . . .*

There are so many people today who have this image
that God is "out there somewhere." In this kind of thinking, God is not here now. He is not with the orphans in
Haiti who cry for His help; He is somewhere else. It's a
mind-set that assumes that God created this world, set it

in motion, and left—waiting to meet us again once the finish line of life is in sight.

But nothing could be further from the truth. In Psalm 139:7-12, the writer wrestles with this kind of perception about God. He says:

> Where can I go from your Spirit?
>> Where can I flee from your presence?
> If I go up to the heavens you are there;
>> if I make my bed in the depths, you are there.
> If I rise on the wings of the dawn,
>> if I settle on the far side of the sea,
> even there your hand will guide me,
>> your right hand will hold me fast.
> If I say, "Surely the darkness will hide me
>> and the light become night around me,"
> even the darkness will not be dark to you;
>> the night will shine like the day
> for darkness is as light to you.

The story of the Scriptures is a story of a God who is ever-present. From the very beginning to the very end, God is a God who is here, now, as close as our next breath. We essentially live in a God-drenched world. Therefore, central to what it means to be a Christian is the belief that God is alive and in every moment, in every place. God is not the God of someday or the God of somewhere else. He is the God of now.

Consider again what the writer of James 1:27 is saying: "Religion that God our Father accepts as pure and faultless is this: to look after the widows and orphans in their distress and to keep oneself from being polluted by the world." Try to imagine a religion that is pure, a religion that is faultless. How many of us care for orphans or widows every day? This kind of language is used in the Scriptures rarely, but here it is in black and white. Do you want to know what kind of life God sees as pure and faultless? Look after the widows and orphans and you're beginning to tap into that kind of life. You're beginning to tap into the heart of God.

What's also fascinating is what the verse does *not* say. The verse *doesn't* say, "Religion that God our Father accepts as pure and faultless is this: Be involved in one more Bible study or more church activities." No, the writer of James envisions something much different. It appears that what is central to being a follower of Jesus is to live a life of selflessness and generosity. It is not an option; it is the Christian life at its very essence.

Micah 6:8 carries this thought a step further. Speaking on behalf of God to his people, Micah calls out, "He has shown all you people what is good. And what does the LORD require of you? To act justly and to love mercy and to walk humbly with your God."

Again, the writer of the book of Micah is trying to convey a message. Do you want to know what kind of life God sees as good? Do you want to know what kind of life He wants you to experience? It is not about keeping up out-ward appearances. It is not about status, or position, or accomplishments. *Act justly and love mercy and walk humbly with your God.*

Clearly, the heart of God is for the marginalized, the poor, the orphan, the widow, and even "the foreigner in your midst."[4] His desire for those who identify themselves with Him is that they would do justice and love doing mercy unto those who are on the margins of society.

All this begs an obvious question: How are we, as a Church, the incarnation of Jesus in this world, living this teaching? Wouldn't it be amazing to see the Church known more for what or who it stands for than for what or who it stands against? Wouldn't it be refreshing to see the Church known more for how it loves because of what it believes than by what it merely says it believes?

Flight attendants, prepare for arrival and cross-check . . .

While the past few weeks had been a whirlwind of activity for the band and a time of transition for Drex and Jo, every time they prepare to go to Haiti, there is this sense that something larger is happening. Like the trips of the past, when Drex and Jo first arrived in Haiti so many years ago, when the band saw the need and decided that they would raise money to build an orphan-age, when they returned to purchase the property or when a youth group from Southern California flew in to help with the construction, today felt like it had a grander purpose.

This was more than just a trip to The Hands and Feet Children's Village. It was a chance to experience a piece of the kingdom of God breaking into this world.

Notes
1. "Haiti: The Developmental Challenge," USAID, January 14, 2005. http://www.usaid.gov/policy/budget/cbj2005/lac/ht.html (accessed July 2006).
2. "Haiti: The Challenges of Poverty Reduction," March 1998, posted at "Statistics on Education and Quality of Life in Haiti," *Beyond Borders*.
3. "Adoption Programs in Haiti and Ethiopia," Adoption Associates Inc. http://www.adoptassoc.com/international/rfom/ (accessed June 2006).
4. For a glimpse of this, see Leviticus 19:9-10; Deuteronomy 24:17-18; Isaiah 1:16-17; Jeremiah 5:26-29; Ezekiel 16:49-50; and Matthew 25:31-46.

Chapter 2
THE SOUNDS OF HOPE

I think it's a cold, cold world
and I think we need to heat it
So go ahead and strike a match
a passionate heart is needed

"START A FIRE"
AUDIO ADRENALINE

As the plane rolls to a stop on the runway and the doors are opened, the first thing that hits you is the heat. It's like a blast from a furnace. Stepping out of the rear exit of the plane and making your way down the staircase, you walk across the tarmac toward the Port-au-Prince International terminal, still trying to breathe. The air is hot and humid—almost stifling. And it's only January.

"You ought to see what this place is like in the middle of summer," Mark says. "Now that's hot!"

Once you arrive at the door of the terminal and get away from the noise of the plane, you hear music. Waiting to greet you, like you've returned home from a long journey, is a five-piece band similar to the ones you would see on just about every street corner in New Orleans during Mardi Gras. Mark stops, smiles, and gives a nod to the guys in the band, as if they are long lost friends. When they reply warmly, Mark says, "I love those guys. They're always here."

It's clear from the moment Mark arrives that he is in his element. Stress and worry seem to evaporate from him when he is here. For him, coming to Haiti is like coming home.

The Journey to Jacmel
Port-au-Prince is located almost in the middle of the country and near the coast. It lends its name to the bay on which it is located, Baie de Port-au-Prince. It's a city of almost two million people, and it serves as the country's capital. Known for its political instability, few people ever

walk around the city after dark. It is rarely a final destination for those coming to the country.

The city is a study in paradox. On the one hand, it is
bustling with colors and activity, filled with traffic and
people. On the other, corruption and violence are com-
monplace. The city spreads from the slum neighborhood
of the coast up to the more affluent neighborhoods of
Pétionville, a suburb of Port-au-Prince located in the surrounding mountainside.

After clearing customs, the group exits the airport to
a flurry of activity. It is midday, and there are people
teeming around the exit doors, trying to wave them over
to their taxis. The group moves past the myriad of people
trying to grab their attention. Once free from the crowd
at the door, they connect with a Haitian man, perhaps in
his thirties, who is to provide their transportation from
the main airport to the "little" airport and the next leg of
the journey.

Six people, their luggage and eight bins are crammed
into an old Toyota van. Will literally lays on top of the bins
in the back because there is no more space to sit. Rolling
away from the airport, the van looks like one of the miniature clown cars from the circus, or a youth ministry exper-
iment of how many people (and things) you can possibly
fit into one vehicle.

The ride from the International airport to the little
airport is no more than five minutes or so, but once you
leave the main airport, you are hit by the second sensa-

tion of the trip—a smell like few things in this world. The air is thick with a pungent combination of trash, tires, wood and other items being burned. It's everywhere. If you have ever smelled it before, you know . . . it is something you will never forget. It takes a few hours or so to become completely acclimated to the smell, but eventually you reach the point that you forget it is even there. In the first five minutes, however, it completely assaults your senses.

Waiting at the little airport in Port-au-Prince is a collection of small single-prop aircraft run by various charter companies. These charter aircraft make up the intra-island transportation that flies between Port-au-Prince and the outlying areas of the country. With The Hands and Feet Project being on the southern coast of Haiti near Jacmel, the choice is either an eight-hour drive along the coast—which, while beautiful, is also quite an unpredictable adventure—or a 15-minute flight over the mountain ranges of south-central Haiti. For time, as well as cost, the $45 per person 15-minute flight is the way to go. However, with all the turbulence you experience, if you've never flown in a small aircraft, it might be the longest 15 minutes of your life.

After taking off, the plane heads directly west over the ocean. The last thing you see of the area of Port-au-Prince is the slum area near the ocean. From the air, it is a sight of poverty like very few in the world. Thousands upon thousands of makeshift shacks with tin roofs are huddled on

A small dwelling outside of Jacmel.
Most houses in Haiti consist of cinder-
block walls and roofs made of tin or
thatched palm branches.

top of each other in random array. The streets, however, are laid out with almost geometric precision.

It is then that the scenery begins to change.

The ocean below, filled with visible reefs and a myriad of shipwrecks—some accidental, others not—is a rich and vibrant hue of blue and green. It is at this point that you remember that Haiti, although known primarily for its extensive poverty, is actually a part of the beautifully diverse Caribbean islands. In fact, it has been said that when Columbus encountered the Caribbean islands, he remarked that the island of Haiti was the most beautiful of all the jewels of the Caribbean.

Banking left and heading due south to the city of Jacmel, the slums of Port-au-Prince give way to splashes of green as the plane skips along the undulating mountain range of southern Haiti. Dotted along the tops of these mountain ranges, as well as on hillsides and in the valleys, is a peculiar collection of cinder block buildings with tin roofs. These are the homes of the Haitian farmers who make their living off the fertile land of the mountains. What stands out, however, is the lack of road access to any of these outlying areas. All that is evident in this area of the country are horse and mule trails. Then all at once, the picture comes into focus: These people have built homes and carry on their trade using these trails to carry supplies via mules or horses.

The other striking feature is that these mountainous regions lack forests. If you were to look east toward the part of the island that is in the Dominican Republic, these same mountainous ranges would be filled with lush forests. The reason for this difference is because one unique feature of Haitian culture is that the people cook their food over burning coals in pits and makeshift barbeques. Very few people have actual kitchens, so most meals are prepared in this fashion. Because of this practice, one item is needed in abundance: coal.

What the Haitian people have done is to develop a way of making coal out of the wood of the trees in the forest area. In the outlying mountain areas, wood is placed within an oven in order to perform a controlled burn. This process chars the wood without consuming it completely. These coals are then brought down to the markets and sold. This practice has been going on for decades, and now one of Haiti's most beautiful natural resources is being used up at an alarming rate.

A Brief History of Haiti

Haiti, with a population of just over eight million, has a staggering unemployment rate of 80 percent.[1] The majority of Haitians live on less than $1 a day, with the median income being only about $60 a year.[2] Only 25 percent of the population has access to safe drinking water, and less than 30 percent of the population has access to adequate sanitation.[3] Just under half of the people in the nation are literate.[4] In addition, the average life expectancy for Haitians is less than 50 years.[5]

Ironically, in colonial times the island was once the richest and most sought-after territory in the Caribbean. At the time of the French Revolution, the island produced nearly 60 percent of the world's coffee supply and almost 40 percent of the sugar imported into France and England. When the nation declared its independence from France in 1804—becoming the second country in the Americas (after the United States) to free itself from a European power—the future looked promising for the people on this small Caribbean isle. However, in the subsequent two centuries, dictators, coups and corrupt governments have served to destabilize the nation and destroy its once thriving economy.

Christopher Columbus first landed on the island in 1492 while searching for the New World. When his flagship, the *Santa María,* struck a reef and sank on Christmas Eve, he established a makeshift settlement on the northern coast. Columbus soon discovered the presence of a native population, the Tainos, on the island. At first the relationship was amicable, but it quickly deteriorated as the Spaniards began to subjugate the Tainos and treat them with intolerance and abuse.

Over the next 30 years, conflicts between the Spaniards and the natives escalated. The Spaniards reduced the Tainos to slavery and massacred huge numbers of the population. In 1520, with the imminent demise of the Tainos—which had been a ready means of slave labor—the Spaniards began importing slaves from Africa.

By 1550, the effects of forced labor, disease and abuse had taken its toll on the native peoples, and only 150 Tainos remained.

Eventually the island was stripped of its rich mineral deposits and fell out of the mother country's concern. However, in 1659, the French realized that the island was of central importance as a gateway to the Caribbean and began to colonize Tortuga Island off the coast of Haiti. In 1670, the French established a community on the northern portion of the mainland, called Cap François (later renamed Cap Haïtien). By 1731, Spain, no longer interested in the island, officially recognized the sovereignty of the French colony and divided the island along the line of two rivers.

Under the French rule, the island soon became the richest and most sought after in the world. Yet the prosperity came at a cost to the African slave population. The French continued to bring in more slaves from Africa, who were subjected to much of the same abuses and mistreatment that the Spaniards had inflicted on the Tainos.

In 1758, the white landowners put forth legislation discriminating against the black population. The legislature forbade the *affranchis*, or *gens de couleur* ("people of color"), from holding certain occupations, intermarrying with the white population, wearing European clothing, carrying swords or firearms in public, or even from attending social events within the white community. The legislation heightened racial tensions and fueled rebellion on the island. Slaves and other members of the black community demanded freedom and equality. All that was needed was a spark to set the whole country ablaze.

That spark came in the form of a slave revolt. On August 22, 1791, the northern portion of the country erupted in violence. In a rage, members of the black community in the northern settlement slaughtered every white person they could find. The carnage was frightful—and reprisal was swift. In the ensuing weeks, an estimated 10,000 blacks and 2,000 whites were killed in the rebellion, and more than 1,000 plantations were completely destroyed.

In 1793, Toussaint Louverture, one of the few literate and educated black revolutionaries, took control of the north-central portion of the island and began winning victories against the French. By 1800, the entire country was effectively under the rule of Toussaint. However, in 1802 Napoleon Bonaparte sent a French force to the island to quell the revolution and restore the French crown. In 1803, Toussaint surrendered and was deported to France.

Toussaint's capture served to rally the Haitian forces. In May 1803, Jean-Jacques Dessalines, one of Toussaint's generals, took over the command of the Haitian forces. The French army, weakened by an outbreak of yellow fever and lacking reinforcements, fell one final time to the black revolutionary army. On January 1, 1804, Dessalines pronounced Haiti independent from France, thus establishing

François "Papa Doc" Duvalier (left)
and his son, Jean-Claude "Baby Doc"
Duvalier (right). During their com-
bined 30-year rule, Haiti became the
poorest nation in the Americas.

the first black republic in history. In honor of the island's first natives, he adopted the original Taino name, *Hayti* ("mountainous land"), for the name of the new republic.

Dessalines crowned himself emperor of Haiti in 1805 and assumed absolute power over the republic. However, while the new republic was celebrated as giving new freedom to the blacks, little actual improvement occurred within the country. Dessalines's reign was rife with tyranny and abuse, which ultimately lead to his assassination on October 17, 1806. After Dessalines's death, the country was divided by civil war until Jean Pierre Boyer again unified the country in 1822. In 1825, Boyer paid 150 million francs to the French crown to have Haiti recognized as an independent nation—an act that served to empty the Haitian treasury.

In 1844, Boyer was overthrown in a revolution, and the country again went through several decades of political instability. In the early 1900s, the United States, fearing the prospects of war in Europe, began searching for naval bases that it could secure in the Caribbean. This led to the invasion of Haiti in 1915 and a U.S. occupation that lasted until 1934.

In 1956, the Haitian history of political unrest and tyranny reached its pinnacle in the person of François Duvalier, known as "Papa Doc." Duvalier was voted president through the support of the black middle class and the growing rural population. He maintained his rule through the implementation of a private militia known as the *tonton macoutes*, named after Haitian folklore about "Uncle Knapsack" (or "*tonton macoutes*") who stole children in the middle of the night using a backpack.

Duvalier's rule was a time of terror in Haiti. During his reign, almost 30,000 Haitians were killed for political reasons. He jailed newspaper editors and radio station owners that disagreed with his policies and terrified the uneducated classes by claiming that he was Baron Samedi, a vodou spirit of the dead. He stole land holdings from the peasants and gave them to officers in his *tonton macoutes* army, initiated building projects to steal money from investors, and appropriated all the foreign aid money that was given to ease the suffering in his country. Intellectuals and educated professionals—the future hope of the country—fled Haiti in droves.

Jean-Claude Duvalier, known as "Baby Doc," took over where his father had left off in 1971. Jean-Claude's leadership resulted in so much civil unrest that he was finally forced to flee to France on February 7, 1986. In his wake, Jean-Claude left behind an unstable country that was being pulled apart at the seams both economically and politically. By the time of Papa Doc and Baby Doc's departure, Haiti had sunk to such an incredible level of poverty that is was considered to be one of the poorest nations in the world.

The political landscape in Haiti continued to be volatile over the next few years as various factions vied for power. In December 1990, a young priest named Father

Jean-Bertrand Aristide was elected president, but political stability remained elusive. Within a year of Aristide's taking office, dissatisfied factions in the army opposed his leadership and forced him into exile. Between 300 and 500 Haitians were killed in the days following the coup. Over the next two years, more than 40,000 Haitians attempted to flee the country.

In October 1994, Aristide was restored to power and returned to Haiti to complete his term in office. In 1996, René Préval, an ally of Aristide, ran for president and was elected with 88 percent of the vote. In 2000, Aristide ran for president again and was elected with 91.8 percent of the vote, but this time a number of political parties contested the validity of the election results. In the conflict that ensued, inflation rates soared to a high of 42.7 percent at the end of 2003, worsening the already appalling living conditions for the people in the country.

In January 2004, a group known as the Revolutionary Artibonite Resistance Front began a revolt against Aristide, capturing several of Haiti's largest cities and splitting the country between the rebels in the north and Aristide's forces in the south. By February 2004, the rebels had advanced to within a few miles of Port-au-Prince, forcing Aristide to once again flee the country on February 29, 2004.[6]

Since then, Haiti has struggled to find stability, both economically as well as politically. The historical landscape of Haiti reveals a people who are hungry for freedom, a people who are filled with life. Haitians are a vibrant people,

An open market in the streets of Jacmel. The market is the center of commerce and also the center of social life in the region.

alive with laughter, warmth and joy. They are a people who are filled with hope in the midst of despair. Despite all they have been through, they believe that their story is not finished yet. They believe that there is a tomorrow still to be written and that things will perhaps be better then.

Life in Jacmel

The cobalt blue ocean appears in the distance as the plane flies over the mountain range of southern Haiti. Although it's been only 15 minutes, the drone of the engine has put the entire team in a reflective, almost meditative mood. As the group looks ahead to the city of Jacmel, the realization of their final destination comes alive.

Hope amidst despair. Light in the darkness. These are the things that Jesus calls us to be. These are the things that The Hands and Feet Project wants to bring to this country and its people—to let them know that there is something more. There is a tomorrow still to be written, and it will be better.

The kingdom of God is afoot in this world.

The wheels of the plane touch down on the "runway" at the Jacmel airport. The runway is paved, although this is a new feature here. Not too long ago, this was a gravel runway in the middle of a field. In fact, it is still not uncommon to see animals crossing the airstrip as well as people on bicycles who try to use it as a shortcut of sorts.

Exiting the plane, the team takes the bins and suitcases and loads them into Drex and Jo's Toyota pickup, which has been awaiting their return to the orphanage. Leaving the gate of the airport, which is opened and closed by a man sitting in a chair by the gate, the pickup makes a left-hand turn, heading east on the main road.

Jacmel is home to nearly 15,000 people. The name of the city, "Jacmel," comes from a Taino word for "rich land." It was a thriving coffee port at the turn of the twentieth century and was also known as a resort location for the very wealthy. To this day, along its harbor, you can still see luxurious Victorian-style mansions and buildings built in the late nineteenth century by the area's wealthy merchants.

The market at Jacmel is the center of everyday life. To walk the market is an experience like few others. Noisy and bustling with life, it is the hub of social life. This is the place where people come every day to buy whatever they need for the day: beans, rice, vegetables, fruits, meat, household items, clothing—even the all-essential wood coals for cooking. All of these items are brought from the surrounding region to be sold here at the market.

Under large canopies, women sit on the ground with a piece of cloth in front of them. These women most likely picked fresh this morning the produce displayed before them on the cloth. Some have an elaborate spread with a variety of choices, while others have just a few offerings.

Perhaps the most intriguing area of the market is the meat area. Here, women crouch at wood chopping blocks on the ground as they cut and separate portions of freshly butchered animals—and even a few who are awaiting such fate! One quick glance and you know that you are far, far away from home. There's a cow's head on a table. Chickens with essential portions of their bodies freshly severed lie nearby. There's a woman trying to cut a hoof of some sort off of a leg of some kind of animal. The entire area is like a scene out of a B-rated horror movie. It is not for the faint of heart.

Without the market, the city of Jacmel, as well as the surrounding area, would not operate. The market is not only the center of commerce but also the center of social life in the region. People talk about the happenings of the city, the politics of the country, and the hope of the future. To see the market is to touch the soul of Jacmel.

If the soul of Jacmel is the market, the carnival is its heart. "Carnival" is a word derived from the Latin *carne vale* meaning "goodbye to flesh." It marks an epic celebration in the days leading up to Ash Wednesday, the first day of Lent, traditionally a time of reflection and repentance. Carnival is the final celebration before the somber days to come. Much like Mardi Gras, also known as "Fat Tuesday," carnival is a time of unbridled passions, celebrated with much gluttony and drinking.

The carnival celebrated in the streets of Jacmel is one of the most elaborate and colorful spectacles in all of Haiti. The area, already known for its exquisite artistry, comes alive in full color. The streets are filled with parades, music, dancing and even miniature theatrical productions. Elaborate masquerade costumes, including Jacmel's trademark

A small farm near The Hands and Feet
Project. Approximately 80 percent of
the rural population in Haiti lives
in abject poverty.

papier-mâché masks, fill the streets and alleys.

Many of the costumes, as well as the theatrical productions, bend everyday reality. Humans dress up as animals; animals are dressed up like humans; men and women cross-dress. Carnival is also a time of social and political commentary in which any and every message is allowed. With biting satire and mockery, the townspeople stage historical reenactments of the slave rebellion and overthrow of the French. One of the standard reenactments performed during carnival includes the *chaloskas*, in which men dress up in black military uniforms with masks of red lips and large teeth. They mockingly symbolize the secret police, the *tonton macoutes*, who terrorized the Haitian population under the reign of Papa Doc Duvalier.

Along with carnival, the vodou religion is central to the spirit of the Haitian people. The term "vodou" comes from a Creole word meaning "ancestral spirit and drums." Practitioners of vodou believe in one God, whom they call *Gran Met*, but also believe in the presence of a lesser entity, called *lwa*, who can be summoned through vodou rituals including prayer, singing and dancing with drums. Once summoned, *lwa* possesses vodou followers, bringing about manifestations of healing and prophecy.

Vodou traces its roots to the animistic spirit religions of the West African people. When slaves were brought from the coasts of West Africa, they also brought their vodou beliefs and practices with them on the slave ships.

Once they reached the New World, their vodou practices were outlawed; so to keep their beliefs alive (as well as please the influx of missionaries in the region), vodou practitioners began to incorporate Catholic icons into their rituals and ceremonies. This syncretism between vodou and Catholicism can still be seen today. While many of the icons used in Catholicism and vodou look the same, the beliefs are radically different, as adherents to vodou see the icons as various forms and expressions of *lwa*.

Aside from being a religion, vodou has also served as a unifying political force for the people of Haiti. Vodou was credited to have been a driving force within the slave rebellion of 1791 and the final push for independence from the French empire in 1803. Since then, many revolutionaries with political aspirations have claimed to be vodou priests.

The World of the Haitian People

Once outside the airport gate, the truck picks up speed. The weather is gorgeous. The almost stifling heat of Port-au-Prince has now become a cool ocean breeze. The unlined street carries vehicle traffic in both ways. *Tap-taps*, trucks that are the Haitian equivalent of taxis, barrel down the road with 30 to 40 people standing and hanging all over them. They are called "tap-taps" due to the tapping required by passengers to let the driver know that they have reached their destination.

Driving in Haiti is an experience all its own. The roads, although not lined, are wide enough for perhaps three lanes of cars, at best. Pedestrians line both sides of the street carrying goods or just socializing by the roadside. Because people line the sides of the main thoroughfare, the shoulders of the roads act as a kind of social gathering point—part transportation, part public cookout—with charcoal grills every hundred yards or so. Survival on the open road necessitates a vigorous use of the horn. Pedestrians walking, tap-taps moving along at the speed of light, and the myriad of motorcycles and scooters moving every which way make driving interesting, to say the least.

Everywhere you look in Haiti, you see signs of widespread poverty. Every few miles or so, a local well can be seen, which is pretty much the only source of running water in the area. Electricity is a luxury that most Haitians cannot afford. In Haiti, if you want to have electricity, the electric company will come out and give you access to the power line, but it is up to you to purchase the pole and transformer as well as figure out how to run the power lines to your house. The price is way beyond what the average Haitian could ever afford.

As the truck leaves the surrounding area of Jacmel, the rural landscape begins to turn lush and tropical. Palm trees, white-sand beaches and banana trees line the road. It's almost hard to fathom the paradox that in a place so beautiful there is so much poverty. Children play soccer in vacant lots. Women walk along the roadside carrying large baskets or bundles on their heads.

It appears to be a world far away, and yet one so close.

The truck slows and makes a left-hand turn onto a nondescript piece of property with a large building halfway under construction. The first floor is complete; the second floor is well underway. The neighborhood children see the truck pull in. Leaving behind all they were playing with, they run toward the truck with large smiles, calling out, "Mark! Mark! Mark!"

Within seconds of pulling around the building, Mark jumps out of the back of the pickup and is swarmed by the neighborhood kids. There are hugs and high fives, laughter and joy.

This is The Hands and Feet Project. This is the sound of hope.

Notes

1. "Statement from Wyclef," *Yele Haiti Foundation*. http://www.yele.org/vision.html (accessed April 5, 2006).

2. "Haiti: The Challenges of Poverty Reduction," March 1998, posted at "Statistics on Education and Quality of Life in Haiti," *Beyond Borders*. http://www.beyondborders.net/statistics.htm (accessed April 5, 2006).

3. "Stats on Haiti," *Unicef*. http://www.unicef.org/media/media_19596.html (accessed April 5, 2006).

4. "Haiti: Demographic Indicators," *Pan American Health Organization*. http://www.paho.org/English/SHA/prflhai.htm (accessed April 5, 2006).

5. "Stats on Haiti," *Unicef*.

6. The historical information in this section is from Conner Gorry and
   Thomas Kohnstamm, *Lonely Planet Caribbean Islands* (Oakland, CA:
   Lonely Planet Publications, 2005); "A Country Study: Haiti," The Library
   of Congress, http://lcweb2.loc.gov/frd/cs/httoc.html (accessed April 5,
   2006); "Background Notes: Haiti, March 1998," U.S. Department of State,
   http://www.state.gov/www/background_notes/haiti_0398_bgn.html
   (accessed April 5, 2006); "Haiti: History," Wikipedia.com, http://en.
   wikipedia.org/wiki/Haiti#History (accessed May 30, 2006); "Synopsis of
   Haitian History," Discover History, http://www.discoverhaiti.com/his
   tory_summary.htm (accessed July 2006); "François 'Papa Doc' Duvalier
   (1907-1971)," The Dictatorship.com, http://www.giles.34sp.com/bio
   graphies/papadoc.htm (accessed July 2006).

Chapter 3

FROM THE PORCH

Let's get foolish,
let's get free
Free to be the one thing
you were meant to be

"DIRTY"
AUDIO ADRENALINE

The nights in Cyvadier are remarkably cool. And just as the heat of the day dissipates into the coolness of the night, so the busyness of the day slows for the surrounding areas. As night falls, the moon is out in full and the faint sound of bugs fills the tropical night with a buzz.

It had been a long day of travel. Dinner was finished, and after the dishes were done, Chris, Mark and Will relaxed on the front porch of the main building at The Hands and Feet Project. After settling into the Haitian wicker furniture, the conversation moved from the events of the day to the dreams for the project.

Hands and Feet (HAF): I'd love to hear about how you guys grew to have a heart for this place.

Will: I'll start. I think it is interesting how years ago God birthed a heart for missions in the bands that Mark and I were in. It began in Bible college. I ran into Mark, who had just been dropped off by his parents, who were heading off to Haiti. It was obvious that they had a heart for missions, and it rubbed off on Mark.

When we formed the band, the idea of missions became such a big part of our records. It was a thread that was always there; something we never got away from. God knew what He was doing. It was that passion and thread that caused us to want to create and support something like The Hands and Feet Project. Then to see Drex and Jo's heart for this, and to see them want to get involved in it—it's amazing. When you sit back and see the big picture, this thread of missions has been such a big part of our lives. It was a passion that fueled us to do what we do.

HAF: What I find amazing is that there are so many people who pick up on various causes, but The Hands and Feet Project isn't just a cause. It feels very different. It's very much a part of who you are, as individuals and as a band.

Mark: People ask me why I do this. For me, it goes even deeper than a calling in that this just feels right for me. I love this place. I don't know what I would do if I were not doing this. When I come here, I start to melt into who I am supposed to be. It's not about sacrificing to come here. In fact, it's really not a sacrifice to me. It is just something that God birthed in me as early as junior high.

Some of my earliest memories of Haiti are filled with a fascination—all of these colors and these beautiful kids. It was just amazing. It was an experience like I'm sure a lot of people have. You go on a trip in junior high or high school to a Third World country, and your eyes are opened. You think, *So this is how the world really lives. This is how the world exists.* It's not as if these people are unlucky or not blessed; it's just different. So from early on, I fell in love with the place. I loved coming here and being a part of what my parents were doing. I think that is what has led me to come back off and on. It's home.

When I think about this place, so much of it is about wanting to get kids to go on trips and to understand the Third World and the need that is out there. It seems like the Church is so absorbed in building things and getting their numbers up, or what their carpet looks like, or what their pews look like. Yet the Church, to really be the Church, needs to be more about community and serving. Our hope is that this place can help the Church become outward-focused rather than inward-focused. Hopefully, after coming here, people can go home and say, "How can we serve our community?" Ultimately, it's about getting people in the Church to serve where they are and where they live to hopefully change the community.

We're not just talking about the island of Haiti; we're talking about something bigger. You don't necessarily have to come with us to Haiti; you can be hands and feet wherever you are. I know how much it changed my life. It gave me perspective. Haiti does that for me.

I remember sitting here the first time we had a group in to work on this building. We did this devotional about the journey we are all on and how it is not so much about the end product or what we accomplish, but that the important part is the journey. Early on, God really laid on my heart that The Hands and Feet Project was going to be about the journey—the everyday things of not only building the buildings, but also working with the people here. And not only the Haitians, but the missionaries who are here as well. It was going to be about embracing the struggles and the successes of everyday living rather than pushing forward to some goal.

I think this project is going to have an incredible impact on kids and is truly going to affect this country. But I also think this will be a place that will change the people who come to sweat and work together and cry and pray together. This is not a place where people will be comfortable. Sometimes, being comfortable is not good. This is a place where people might be afraid or scared, seeing babies who are hungry and dying. Yet in the midst of it, God might deal with their heart, perhaps by dealing with something they've been wrestling with for years. I've seen it happen. It changes people. It changes whole churches.

HAF: How did The Hands and Feet Project get started? How did the idea first come up?

Mark: It actually came from the song "Hands and Feet" more than anything else. I was sitting in my living room watching CNN one night and saw a story about a mudslide in Mexico that killed 6,000 or 7,000 people. It was 1998 or 1999. I just sat there thinking, *What are we supposed to do? How can we help?* It was just so overwhelming; you just feel helpless.

So I wrote the song "Hands and Feet" from that place of wanting to do something. I really wanted to empower people with that song—that you truly can make a difference in people's lives. It's more than just about passing out tracts or preaching; it's about getting out there and becoming the hands of Jesus to touch people, the way He touched people.

After the song "Hands and Feet," we did a whole record about missions called *Worldwide*. It was at a time when the whole worship side of Christian music was taking off. We didn't feel like we wanted to put out a worship album, because we really didn't feel like that is what we were supposed to do. It wasn't true to who we were.

At that time, everyone in the band was listening to different preachers and going to different churches. Yet we all were reading and hearing about the concept that worship was more than just singing a song; it was about sacrificing and giving God everything. We decided to make a record about worshiping God with our life, and that's where the record *Worldwide* came in. All the songs were about doing something besides just sitting in a church pew—getting out there and getting your hands dirty as a way of worshiping God.

So after the record was out, we did a tour called The Go Show with Mercy Me. We had nearly 5,000 kids come forward over the course of the entire tour and commit to go on a short-term missions trip. It was amazing. We also started a thing called The Go Foundation with Mercy Me, a foundation that has sent kids on missions trips around the world.

Then fast-forward a bit. We started to sense that we wanted to build something ourselves and really get

Mark Stuart unloads his bag outside
of the airport in Port-au-Prince.

involved. There are missionaries I know who are on the mission field because of how God used some of our songs, which is amazing. But [The Hands and Feet Project] was something for us to do individually. It was something we could do as Audio Adrenaline. We wanted to go out, raise the money, go to Haiti and build it with others. It was something we wanted to invest in personally. We wanted our kids to be a part of it someday.

At the same time, Bob Herdman, who was on the road with Audio Adrenaline, was thinking the same thing. He was running Flicker Records, and he came to us and said, "I really want to start something and get my church involved." What was funny was that early in 1991, Bob and I had made a trip to Haiti and were in Port-au-Prince the whole time. For Bob, it was one of the worst experiences he had ever had. I remember him saying, "I'm never going back there again." Yet years later, here he was, saying, "I think we need to go back to Haiti and build an orphanage." It was August 2004, and we were standing right over there by the truck. We bought the land without any kind of support.

Since then, as we've shared the dream about The Hands and Feet Project, people have responded. It's crazy. There are people all over who are getting behind this project, from giving money to coming down here to help. Whether they have the ability or not to come here, people want to be about helping others. It's truly amazing what God has done.

So that's pretty much how it started. It's been about people feeling the call of James 1:27—to not be about church or religion as much as being about helping orphans and widows.

HAF: Is that the verse that launched the idea of an orphanage ministry?

Mark: It definitely encouraged us to reach out to kids, especially kids in need. We felt that in order to reach the country long-term, we needed to raise up a generation of kids by letting them know what it's like to be loved and to experience the love of Christ from an early age. The generation of kids that we invest in here will hopefully affect a multitude. So the idea came out of a desire to actually invest in the future of Haiti. Even economically, we want to make an impact. We want to have a computer-training program, a mechanical-training program, and a construction-training program—all to give these kids a shot at having something to do with their lives.

HAF: Mark, earlier you talked about how this project has changed your perspective. How so?

Mark: I think that being in a rock band is such a plastic world. It molds you in ways that you don't even realize. It's like you're getting cooked in a pot of water. Slowly, the temperature increases, and all the while you don't even know it's happening until it's too late. It's too easy to look in the mirror one day and find out that you've changed in ways that you never saw coming.

You know, like with Audio we would show up to the bus the night before a show, and it's stocked with all of our favorite drinks, all on ice, and all of our favorite snacks. There's a satellite TV and our bunks. Someone drives us to the venue, where someone else sets up all of our gear that morning.

We go in, and there's lunch prepared for us. Then after lunch, we head out to the mall, or go shopping for the afternoon or go see a movie or something. Then we come back and eat dinner, which has been completely prepared for us. Then we do the show, after which the whole process begins again. Don't get me wrong; I love what we do. It is difficult always being away and traveling, though. Eventually you lose perspective of what life really is all about.

To be completely honest, I think we've definitely been stuck in that "rock band" rut before. Even as a Christian rock band, you can still become self-absorbed and selfish. It's like so much of the American dream or the American life. It's all about answering the question, What can I do to make my life more comfortable? In our search to answer that question, we can become so detached from how the rest of the world lives. It's insane. I think that, as a band, we were served so much that one day we awoke to what was going on and said it was time for us to serve others.

HAF: Did you sense all along that you were losing perspective, or was it this awakening one day?

Mark: I don't know. I would say something that really rocked my world happened when we were talking about this children's village for the very first time. I was talking to my dad about coming down here and what it would take for them to make it financially. He said that all they needed was about $15,000 a year for them to live on and pay their bills. I asked him, "Why not raise some support and get up to $25,000 a year to continue to pay off your house in Kentucky?" He looked at me like I was speaking another language or something. I can still remember it. He said, "Money? Why do I need money?"

He wasn't being pretentious; he was just saying that he didn't need any more money than just what he needed to live on. It was just so stunning to me. It's so easy to find yourself caught up in stuff that just doesn't matter in the long run. I'm by no means rich, but I guess in a certain perspective I really am. I think I was worrying about my future in regard to being comfortable and what I'm going to do after Audio Adrenaline. Yet the Scriptures tell us not to worry about it; God will take care of us. So there I was talking with my dad about this place, and God stepped in and rocked my perspective on everything.

Will: Yeah, I agree. I think one of the greatest things we need as people is to get out of that search for comfort. I think coming here does that. You see what little people can have and live with, yet be so contented and so happy. It rocks your world. It makes you want to sell everything, you know? It messes with your mind and really puts things in perspective.

Mark: I think it's ironic, too, in that when I was younger, I remember praying all the time for some kind of platform. I don't even know why. I just prayed for a platform to be able to share the good news of God. As I look back now, Audio Adrenaline is a miracle. It's a miracle that it even exists, or that the band even got a record deal, much less that God used it to make an impact. It's been an incredible journey.

I think our desire has always been to be a band that was spurring along youth groups and churches to risk everything—not to just accept how things are, but to challenge the status quo. I think God put that on our hearts when we were in Bible college.

Now that we're older, I think that one of the dreams I would love to see happen is to see people in the Church, in general, be looked at as heroes. I want to see people look back on the times of need, in countries like Haiti, and say, "You know, if it weren't for Christians, or the Church, I don't know what would have happened." I'd love to see that with the AIDS crisis in Africa as well.

There are people doing it. I remember Bono coming to talk to a gathering of Christian artists about what he's doing in Africa with debt relief and the AIDS crisis. His challenge really spoke to people, and it spurred quite a few people to dream and act. I know that Jars of Clay started Blood Water Mission because of it. How amazing would it be to look back on the AIDS crisis and what's happened in these Third World countries and be able to say that these are the people who came to the rescue, these followers of Jesus? It would be incredible—the Church doing and being what the Church is supposed to do and be in this world.

HAF: Was there anything else that Bono said that resonated with you?

Will: One thing Mark communicated to me after he heard Bono speak was that any kind of humanitarian work should come first from the Church, which should then spur along the rest of the world to get involved. That really spoke to me; it was like a wake-up call. It's like as a Church, we've fallen asleep, or have had our heads stuck in the dirt. The Church seems so caught up with so many things that truly don't matter, and I think the world is watching. We need to be the champions who lead the rest of the world in doing great humanitarian acts. We need to be the ones standing up against social injustices—not waiting for the world to act, but acting first ourselves, leading the way. The world is watching, but I think all they see right now is a Church that is fragmented, disjointed and dysfunctional.

HAF: It sounds as if what Bono was calling for was for the Church to reclaim its mission.

Will: I think it goes back to the Early Church in Acts. I just reread the book of Acts, and it paints this beautiful picture of the Church. When you read that there were some who sold what they had to make sure others had what they needed, and that there was no need among them, it just makes you wonder. Then you read that the Lord was adding to their numbers daily. You just get this overwhelming sense of the love and compassion that they had for each other and those outside their community. It was because of this compassion and love that God was adding people to their numbers.

Then you come here, and God just brings those verses to light, especially with the kids. They will come up to a complete stranger and want to hold their hand, or give them hugs, or just cling all over them. It breaks your heart. You wish the Church could see that it's about the needs of those who don't have a lot versus the bigger buildings, or the numbers, or the budget, or the status they have within the community. It's about the people who have needs—the people who get overlooked. It's about the unwed mothers and the poor who are in your midst. What are you doing about them? Like the song "Hands and Feet," it's so basic, and yet so difficult for some people to get their minds around.

HAF: Why do you think it's tough for churches to do that?

Mark: I think it's tougher in America than in other countries because, again, I think in America church has been about cleaning people up, making things look pretty,

Mark and several short-term missionaries
give baby Jabez a bath on the site of
The Hands and Feet Project.

making it comfortable and easy and safe. Church in America is all about being safe, but the church should be a place that is unsafe. It should be kind of scary, because we might be asked to sacrifice, to meet someone's need, to go downtown and cook for someone, or take in an orphan.

Church should be intimidating, and I think that's where the Church in America has lost it. We tend to make it so easy for people and so comfortable that it's almost not even useful anymore. It's a great place to go, relax, worship God and feel good. Yet it doesn't look much like the Church in the book of Acts to me. I mean, they came together and broke bread and sang songs and encouraged one another and exhorted the Scripture, and it was at people's houses. It was more about meeting people's needs than making things comfortable.

HAF: When you think about the future of The Hands and Feet Project, what do you see?

Mark: When I think about the future, I start to see the bigness of this project. One of the things that is shocking to me is the fact that these orphans we're taking in—these beautiful kids that are going to be with us for 17 or 18 years—will be a part of my life for the rest of my life. In fact, it's probably going to take Will's kids and my kids to see this through, to keep it going and growing. There's a part of me that is frightened by that, and a part of me that is excited about the risk factor and the mystery of what this is going to be. It is intimidating, but I think that's a part of being hands and feet—stepping out in faith, risking, investing for a lifetime, not just for a moment. Audio Adrenaline is a thing for the moment. This project is for a lifetime.

Also, I think one of our future goals is to see other Christian artists invest in other places around the world where they feel called. Hopefully, The Hands and Feet Project can be a part of helping make that happen. We would love to help other Christian artists connect with their fans to do something physical and brutal and even scary—like take on an orphanage in Romania or somewhere in Africa. Hopefully, what we've done here will encourage other artists to get involved in something.

Christian music can become stale, superficial and formulaic. What we need are Christian artists who are real and honest making music that is real and honest and transparent. There is such a platform there. Hopefully, The Hands and Feet Project will continue to encourage these younger, edgier bands to communicate to this generation not to grow up and become comfortable and sedate, but to take risks, be dangerous.

I think that's what I want The Hands and Feet Project to stand for—to challenge people to get out of their comfort zone and do something, to live dangerously. We've been created for so much more. There's a line in a movie, I can't remember which one, but it says, "Your heart is free. Let's pray you have the courage to follow it." We have been given freedom in Christ, but how many people live like they're free? The freedom of Christ should look like rock bands in orphanages. I hope that when people think about Audio Adrenaline down the road, they don't just think about the songs or gold records, but they think of a band that took risks or was even a little bit crazy. I think that's what the Early Church was about in the book of Acts. We need people who will be hardcore at being compassionate, loving and meeting needs.

Music has been an incredible tool. God created it, and we used it. We sucked the marrow out of it—we really did, every ounce, man, to the very end—and it was great. I want kids to have that opportunity to live like we lived and like we're living now, to stick it out there and go for it. Live in a van for a while or live in a shack in a Third World country. Life is too short to sit in a pew.

Will: It's so ironic to talk to people about all this. They look at you like you're crazy, but in reality it's them who are crazy. We don't know what we're missing by not stepping out there and letting God do things that we can't even imagine. It seems like we want to hold on to the life we have so badly, we're clutching on to . . .

Mark: . . . to the things that don't really matter.

Will: Yeah, and when you come here, your vision gets broader and deeper. You see how things really are. Then when you go back to the States, it's almost like a culture shock. You can so easily fall back into that mode of living again, where it is all about the busyness of life.

Mark: I think some people look at short-term missions and think, *I could never do that.* There's something about being on a missions trip that's different. It's not torture; it's actually beautiful. Your stress just drips off your body. With every drop of sweat, you forget about all the stuff you cling to that's so meaningless in the bigger picture, the bigger story of life. I don't know; it's almost foolish not to do something like this. I know some people may look at it and say, "You're a fool." Yet to me, the fools are the people sitting in the States not even thinking about taking risks or giving of themselves. They are just thinking about themselves. They are the fools.

Will: I think it's like the rich person who came to Jesus and asked, "How do I get to heaven?" And Jesus said, "Sell all your stuff and come follow Me," and the man went away sad.

Mark: He missed out.

Will: Yeah, he missed out. Something else important is that when you come to places such as Haiti, it's not like you come here because it frees you up from guilt so you can say you did your job and then go back home to your life. You don't come here so you can go back home and be thankful for everything you have because you've felt sorry for the kids here who have nothing. The truth is that even though they may not have what you have, they are so happy and have everything they need. They are some of the most loving people you will ever meet. So maybe it's not them who are poor—maybe it's you. Maybe you need them more than you know.

We had this pastor who said to us one time that we should pray for the gift of tears. That has always stuck with me. It's like when we were on stage and looking into the crowd, I would always think about the people—trying to sense their hurts and their needs, trying to sense what they were going through and how maybe in some way to connect with those hurts and needs. I think that's true of here as well. When you're out of the rhythm of your busy life, you can touch people's hurts and needs. I think that's what being a Christian is all about.

HAF: I heard it said once that when you get out of your routine and you get into a place that stretches you and you look in the faces of the people, it's like a mirror into your soul. So being here and looking into the faces of the people here, what do you see about yourself in that mirror?

Mark: I see some good things and some bad things. I definitely recognize that a big part of my day in the States is wrapped up in how to make my life better. Period, And it's been like that for a while. Bottom line, I just see my self-ishness. I mean, if someone asks me to do something, I'll do it. If somebody needs help, I'll jump in to help. But if I were being honest though, I just feel that I'm looking out for me most of the time.

But when I'm here, something is different. I'm different. Since I've been over here the last year and a half or so, I think I've been different at home, too. I've really been challenged in who I am and where I'm going in life. I think being here has helped change me in that as well. When I'm here, I realize that I'm okay. Yeah, I have some issues, but God's changing me.

Will: For me, I think being here has showed me just how busy I really am. You don't even know how stressed you are in the States. You almost embrace the adrenaline, and then when you come here, you see the people. You see them living in a hut with a mud floor and a thatched roof, and there's a sense of happiness and contentment. It definitely makes you take a deeper look at your life and what makes you tick. It has a way of exposing your motivations.

I think being here is therapeutic for my soul, to be honest. It's like when the band used to do 180 shows a year. When I went home, I loved just mowing my grass—that was like therapy for me. Just to have that hour of normalcy. It was a reminder of what was really real in life. I have grass, and I need to mow it. This is similar. Yet this is way deeper, way more therapeutic in the spiritual sense. It puts me in touch with what really matters.

HAF: I think what I see in the mirror is the reality of the things I worry about and the things I invest myself in. Are those the things I should really be worrying about? Are those the things I should be investing in? Are those really the things . . .

Mark: That should consume you?

Will: Yeah, it's like I'm living in a world filled with "could have" or "should have" or "might have been." I don't want to get to the end of my life and have God say, "There was so much more to the kind of life I intended for you." I feel like when I'm here, I get this sense that I'm somehow living more in tune with how God wants me to live.

I think that's where true peace comes from. I think the reality is that when you are doing the things that Jesus did, you are more in tune with His spirit than you even realize. I think that is what Jesus means in John 10:10 when He says that He came to give us life more abundantly. Or, as one translator said, real and eternal life, more and better than you ever dreamed.

Mark: I think the farther you are from being caught up in yourself or the things that make you comfortable, that's when you really see what life is all about. Once you let go of the computerized, compartmentalized American life, you can come here and breathe deeply.

Chapter 4

HOPE AMIDST DESPAIR

May God bless you with anger at injustice,
oppression, and exploitation of people,
so that you may work for
injustice, freedom and peace

FRANCISCAN BENEDICTION

There is one paved road in the southern part of Haiti just outside of Jacmel that winds down through the lush Haitian jungle. Palm trees jut out on either side of the road, and rocks and scattered undergrowth line the roadway. Often, you will see Drex and Jo Stuart's white pickup truck traveling down this road, ferrying people from the airport to The Hands and Feet Project Children's Village.

As the truck nears the building, children come out to the road and run alongside the pickup, all giggles and toothy white smiles. Eventually, one or two will hop in the back of the truck to ride the rest of the way to the Project building.

Drex, Jo and Chris Cotton, The Hands and Feet Project's executive director, have made friends with many of their neighbors. As a result, a number of the kids in the area now know their names, and when the truck nears, the kids call out the name of the person they see in the back of the truck. Chris says that he carries candy in his pockets for the moment when he hears the local kids start to yell out, "Chris! Chris!"

As the truck continues down the road, a white two-story building comes into view. The building is easily recognizable by its striking columns and wraparound porch that circles the structure on two floors. It is modern on the outside, but constructed in a Haitian style so that it blends into the surrounding area.

In Haiti, a person who buys a piece of land will often build a wall around it first before he or she builds anything

Local workers and short-term missions volunteers helped build the wall surrounding the property (above) and the first floor of the main building (below). The Hands and Feet Project took in their first orphans in late 2005.

else. So on The Hands and Feet Project site, walls line the building on either side, with enough room left on the right side so that a car can drive into the back. The wall extends around the entire three-and-a-half-acre property.

In Haitian communities, all the neighborhood kids play in each other's houses and on each other's land. It is no different at The Hands and Feet Project: Neighborhood kids play in and around the building, sit on the porch, and talk to the short-term missions teams that come and stay for a week or two. There are so many kids around that Drex, Jo and Chris have often dreamed about setting up some kind of youth group in the near future that would minister to the local youth. ("One thing at a time," they say.)

The actual building sits right off of the paved road near the front of the property. Blue rocking chairs line the porch outside the first floor. Even though the building was under construction for a long time and was only recently finished, the porch has always served its purpose as an area for conversation and reflection. On the front left-hand side of the building, a simple concrete stairway reaches out from the first floor to the second floor.

The interior of the first floor is spacious. Once inside, it quickly becomes apparent that the building has many amenities not found in other Haitian homes in the area. For instance, most homes do not have electricity or running water, and 90 percent of Haitians do not have ovens or stoves. Meals are cooked over open fires, and families buy bread, or anything else that has to be baked, at the local baker's shop. However, because The Hands and Feet Project Children's Village is meant to house not only children, nannies and staff such as Drex and Jo but also short-term missions teams, it has electricity, ceiling fans, access to the Internet and even an oven. Water is even readily available from a well located on the property.

To accommodate the many groups that travel to Haiti to work on the Project, the first floor of the building has four bedrooms, four bathrooms, a kitchen and a large communal space that acts as both a dining room and a living room. On the second floor are Drex and Jo's room, a bathroom, and several other rooms. One of these rooms is currently occupied by Edaline, the first nanny employed by The Hands and Feet Project, and her eight-year-old son. Thamara and Jabez, the Project's first two orphans, also live upstairs in a room that they share.

The property on which the building sits backs up to the foothills of a small mountain. So far, in addition to the main building, the property has a water well, a small shed (which houses a generator), and a beautiful, sprawling garden created by Carlos, the Haitian handyman employed by the Project to help maintain both the property and the building. On the remaining land, the team is preparing to build a small open-air chapel and at least three small additional homes that will be dedicated entirely to caring for children. According to Chris, the team is building at least 3 houses and upwards of 10 houses eventually. Each house will be built as a single-story home but with the possibility of adding on second stories to each structure should it become necessary to house more orphans. As of 2006, builders are already laying the foundation for the very first home.

The Plight of the Orphans in Haiti

It's easy to look at the needs of orphans in Haiti and wonder, "What can I do? I'm only one person, living far away." It's easy to be blinded to all that you can do because of the immensity of the need. But it all begins with one child.

Standing on the second floor of the main building, as a handful of Haitian workers plaster the walls and ceiling, putting the finishing touches on a building that is already housing orphans, it's exciting to see the dream starting to take shape. Nearby, Drex surveys the work that needs to be accomplished that day.

"You know, we might not be the best solution, but we might be the only solution the kids who come here will ever have," he says. "This may be their last and only hope. Without something like this, they might possibly die. If this is the last rope they can grab a hold of before they fall over the edge, we want to be that for them. We want to take care of the kids who no one wants or can take care of."

The actual parcel of land on which The Hands and Feet Project is located was purchased from a Haitian family in August 2004. "Land is precious here," Drex says. "Sometimes it is all you have. So the family that we bought it from took some time to think about it before selling it to us. We had to go to each and every family member to have him or her sign off on the sale of the land, just to make it legal.

"On the flight home, after the purchase was finalized, Mark started drawing up plans for the site on a piece of paper. He then gave the plans to our niece, who is an architect. She drew up the official building plans for us. Pretty quickly, we laid the foundations for the wall around the property as well as the foundation for this building. By March 2005, the building itself was well underway. Various groups came in to help with the project at that time. By July 2005, the first floor of this building was complete. We had a group come in from California to help move us in. They painted the walls, hung the doors, built the bunk beds, and even finished the bathrooms."

From the very beginning, The Hands and Feet Project has been about providing a loving, nurturing environment for the orphans of Haiti. By providing the necessary food, clothing, medical attention and care that the children of Haiti so desperately need, the team hopes to save the lives of countless orphans.

Yet there's a larger story going on here. "We don't want to raise these kids to be American," Chris explains. "We want to raise them to be Haitian. We don't want to see them grow up and leave for a better life somewhere else. We want them to stay here and make a better life for the country of Haiti. Haiti will never change if people who are Christian or who are educated leave the country. It will

When Drex and Jo's white pickup arrives at
The Hands and Feet site, local kids will
often run alongside the vehicle to greet
those inside.

only get better if these Haitian orphans grow up to be Haitians and make an impact on this country. We want to be a part of that solution. We truly believe that if we can provide a loving, Christian environment, these orphans can change the future of Haiti."

The life of an orphan in Haiti is dire indeed. There are approximately 450,000 orphans in the country of Haiti, 75,000 of whom are "double orphans," meaning that both of their parents have died. Forty-three percent of all orphans have been orphaned because their parents died of AIDS.[1]

At the heart of the issue is a lack of basic medical care. Disease and other medically treatable issues are rampant across the country. Pregnant mothers in Haiti, especially those living in outlying areas or those in the mountains, rarely get any form of medical attention prior to giving birth. Mothers often give birth at home, using a concrete block to sit on. The husband, if he is still around, sits behind the mother and holds on to her as she pushes. Rags are placed on mud or concrete floors to receive the child when he or she is born. Often, a piece of glass is used to cut the umbilical cord, which in many cases leads to infection. Many children become orphaned at birth because their mothers die from such infections or other complications during the childbirth process.

Regardless of whether the child is orphaned or not, he or she will suffer the effects of malnutrition and the lack of basic medical care. By age four, children begin to develop a reddish tint to their hair, which indicates a vitamin deficiency—a telltale sign of the first stages of malnutrition. Their eyes may become glassy and their stomachs (and other parts of their bodies) may begin to swell. More severe side effects soon follow: heart, kidney and breathing problems develop; the ability to fight off infection and heal is reduced; and various forms of brain damage can also occur due to the lack of nourishment.[2]

All of this leads to some staggering statistics regarding the plight of children in Haiti:

- Nearly 8 percent of all children born in Haiti will die before their first birthday—a rate nearly double that of any other place in the world.
- 21 percent of the children born in Haiti will have a low birth-weight.
- 30,000 children under the age of 5 will die each year.[3]

In most cases, if a child is orphaned, the immediate family will take in that child. Although at first this might sound beneficial, in many cases it is anything but good for the welfare of the child. Often when the immediate family steps in to take the child, they see the child not as a full member of the family but as a commodity or resource. In some cases, the child is made into a kind of indentured servant for the family and is made to do various household chores while the rest of the children are in school. Sadly, school is often just not an option for orphaned children. Sadder still, there are reported cases in which the family will intentionally break the legs of an orphan, allow the bones to heal improperly, and then send the children into the street to beg.

This is the life of an orphan in Haiti—a life in need of hope.

"This is the reason we wanted to start The Hands and Feet Project," Drex states as he inspects a room on the second floor of the building. "We want to be there for these babies. And this building is a big part of that dream."

The Greater Goal of the Project
To conduct the day-to-day operations of The Hands and Feet Project, the team intends to hire Haitian nannies and surrogate parents to live and work with three to six children at a time. By doing so, they hope to be able to raise the children in a loving, stable environment. The team found their first nanny in Edaline, a Christian woman whose husband left her several years ago alone with a child. Edaline has a passion to care for orphans. She is already caring for Thamara and Jabez, and she is ready to care for more. The team plans for her to be the first nanny to move into one of the additional houses being built on the property.

"Originally, we thought, *How in the world are we going to find trustworthy nannies?*" Chris says about their plan. "But it's just happened. We've been blessed to have Edaline come to us. We knew that getting kids would not be a problem, so getting people to care for them would be our biggest unknown, and God has provided. We just have to continue to trust and pray that God will bring the people we need."

For Drex and Jo, the challenge now becomes taking on multiple roles as more kids come under their care. In addition to continuing in their roles as missionaries and construction foremen, they will soon also have to become the primary caregivers and spiritual leaders of the orphans and staff. Yet as challenging as that might seem, they're both excited to finally be able to care for orphans in need.

The team also dreams of seeing the community changed, with community-wide feeding programs, job training, medical and dental care and also the youth-group outreach. "The main goal," remarks Chris, "is to ensure that this has little to do with us as individuals but to make it viable far beyond any of us. We want to see this continue to bring change way beyond our lifetime."

This change has already begun through the relationships the team has formed with individuals in the community, such as the woman who owns the small hardware store, the man who owns the nearby restaurant, the mayor of the little town, and the dozens of laborers and carpenters that The Hands and Feet Project has employed. Some of these folks already come to a regular Bible study with Drex and Jo.

Yet The Hands and Feet Project seeks an even greater goal than just caring for the orphans of Haiti. The team also wants to establish a place that invites others into the journey of understanding what it means to be the hands and feet of Jesus in this world. The Project is about providing an opportunity for people to come from the United States and elsewhere and have their perspective altered. "I don't think you can leave Haiti without your own personal view of life changed—your own morality changed," says Chris. "Coming to a place like Haiti changes your view of what your responsibility is to the world, not just here, but also at home."

Short-term missions teams from all over the United States have already come to the project site to help with construction and to get the land situated for more people to live there. Chris says that in the future, he would like to see teams come down to conduct Vacation Bible Study programs for the orphans who live on-site and for the local kids. And there will be ongoing construction projects for years as more and more kids are taken in.

"We want to invite people into an opportunity to see what life is really like, to take off the blinders of living in America," Chris says. "We want to see people get out of their Christian bubble and learn what it means to serve. Our responsibility as followers of Jesus to this world is so much larger than merely sitting inside a church building on Sunday."

Chris is the perfect example of what he is talking about. When you ask him about how he became involved in the Project, he will simply tell you, "By accident."

Chris knew some friends who were going to Nashville to visit a friend, Mark Stuart. He didn't know Mark at the time, but when his friends asked him if he wanted to go along, Chris agreed. When the group reached Nashville, Mark asked Chris if he wanted to go to his church to hear his parents speak about The Hands and Feet Project. Chris went with Mark to the church and listened to the presentation.

Afterward, Mark and his parents and a few others got together to talk about the progress of the Project, and Chris tagged along. During the course of the meeting, Drex and Jo had a few legal questions that they had no idea how to answer. At the time, Chris, who is a lawyer himself, worked for a nonprofit organization in Los Angeles and had dealt with similar legal questions, so he knew exactly what Drex and Jo needed to do to resolve the issues they were facing.

At the end of the evening, Drex and Jo asked Chris to come down to Haiti and view the Project firsthand. He told them that he would have to raise the funds to get there, but that if he could manage to raise the funds, he would come to Haiti to check out what they were doing there. "I left the next day, not really thinking much about it," Chris recalls.

When Chris returned home, he received a phone call from his best friend in Los Angeles, who was getting married. The friend wanted Chris to be in his wedding and asked him what his schedule looked like over the next few months. "I told him that I had this opportunity to go to Haiti, but I needed to raise $1,000 to be able to do it," Chris says. "My friend said, 'One-thousand dollars, huh? Well, don't worry about it. I sat down last night to look at my giving, and I realized that I had some extra money to give to whatever came up. It was $1,000.' So I went down to Haiti."

Chris had visited many Third World countries before, so getting off of the airplane in Port-au-Prince was not that shocking. "But when we got down to Jacmel and Cyvadier and saw the poverty, it was a different story," he says. "It was like another world. It just staggered me that within an hour and a half of the United States, there was a place like this—a place where kids had barely enough to eat, barely any clothes to wear. I saw kids with reddish hair and distended bellies living in concrete huts with dirt floors and either palm branches or thin sheets of tin for a roof. I was just shaken."

The trip changed Chris's life. "It started to lead me down a completely different path than I was heading down—a different career path, different goals in life," Chris says. "When I look back on it, it's just crazy, really. It impacted me instantly. The minute I went down there, I knew I wanted to be involved. I had to be involved. These kids needed, well . . . hope."

Hope.

If you stop to think about it, hope is the seed of what makes living possible in the midst of the impossible. Hope is looking in the face of what seems to be overwhelming circumstances and saying, "This is not the end of the story." When we believe that what we see is all that there is or all that there ever will be, we live an imprisoned life. But when we embrace hope for the future, the things that oppress us no longer have any power over us. Where there is hope, there is freedom. The kingdom of God comes near, and all the rules change. As one writer put it, "When the kingdom of God comes near, when we experience it, the word impossible deconstructs. It melts and evaporates, and its tyranny over us ends."[4]

The First Orphans: Thamara and Jabez

Hope. Freedom. Change. These are the ideas that drive the mission of The Hands and Feet Project. And they are more than just lofty goals for someday down the road— these ideas are what give breath and life to the everyday life of the Project.

If you spend any amount of time with Mark, Will, Drex, Jo or Chris, you are immediately struck by the realization that they truly believe that through this Project they can alter the lives of many Haitian orphans. They can see the hope amidst the despair—the kind of hope that displays itself in tangible ways.

The hope for each and every orphan can be summed up in the story of two young orphans named Thamara and Jabez. Thamara came to the Project in the fall of 2005 while the main building was still under construction. The team was not yet ready to bring in any children at that point, so

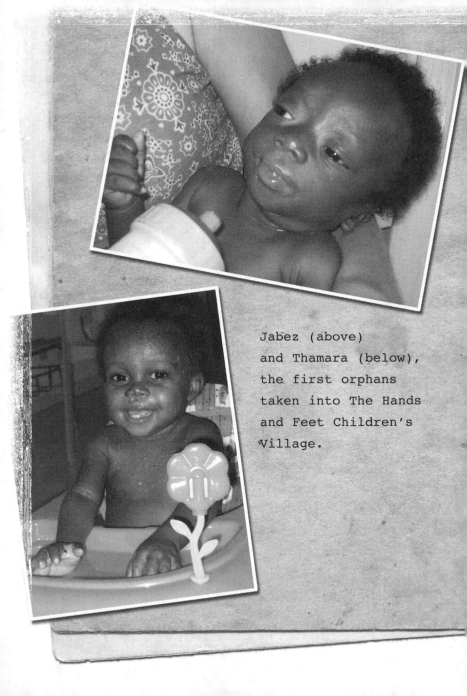

Jabez (above) and Thamara (below), the first orphans taken into The Hands and Feet Children's Village.

when someone brought in this tiny malnourished little baby girl, Chris decided that she could only stay for the night. Christ says that he tried to play the "tough boss" and not commit to taking on any orphans until he felt they were fully prepared. But God had other plans.

Thamara's mother had passed away from complications related to childbirth a few months after Thamara was born, and Thamara's father didn't want to have anything to do with raising a child, so he simply left her. A neighbor and friend near the Children's Village agreed to care for Thamara with help from the Project team while Drex and Jo and others finished construction of the main building; a church in Kentucky became Thamara's sponsor and paid for her room and board. Thamara is now a happy, chattering, two-and-a-half-year-old little girl who "eats like a champ," says Chris.

"My hope for Thamara is that she would grow up to love Jesus and to be His follower," says Jo. "I want her to have the opportunity to go to school and receive an education. I want her to be independent, to support herself and to have a sense of security in who she is—a sense of dignity. I want to see her be able to have a future, a bright one."

"I want to see her become independent, have a family of her own and be able to raise them," Drex adds. "I want her to feel that she could come back at anytime to The Hands and Feet Project and sense that this is family, this is home. I want her to see this place not as something that got her through, but that it was a transformational part of her story—it gave her hope, it gave her dignity, it gave her the tools to function as a participant in society. Basically, I want her to see that it gave her an opportunity to really live."

Jabez's story is not unlike Thamara's. One day, some missionary friends of The Hands and Feet Project who work in a clinic up in the mountain area of Seguin told Drex, Jo and Chris about a baby boy who had been stuck in his mother's birth canal for almost 12 hours. Due to the strain of the birth, his mother died.

After the child was born, everyone thought he would be severely mentally and physically deformed. When the team first saw Jabez, he was very small, underweight and looked to have a major defect on the right side of his face and body, as if he had had a stroke. For the first few months of his life, he never even moved the right side of his body or face.

The missionaries asked Drex, Jo and Chris if they could take in the baby boy and care for him. Again, as with Thamara, the building was not yet ready to house anyone, let alone a potentially handicapped newborn. So the missionaries and The Hands and Feet Project team teamed up and took care of Jabez for a few months until he could be brought into the building with Thamara and Edaline.

Today, Jabez is fully mobile; he can use his right side almost as freely as his left, and he can also respond to people and say his own name. Recently, a nursing group came through the area and gave Jabez a check-up. They reported that he has made major progress and has a good shot at living a fairly normal life.

"We didn't expect to take on a physically or mentally handicapped kid right away," Chris says. "But often, kids like that in Haiti will die because parents simply won't take care of them and there's no prenatal care at all in the hospitals. Throughout Haiti, you don't see many handicapped people because, honestly, they just don't survive childhood."

The Story of Jonas

Many of the stories of Haiti's orphans don't end as happily.

Recently, with the completion of the main building, Drex and Jo decided that they could take in more children. Their friend Teresa, the same missionary who had brought them Jabez, told them to go check the local hospital as it is a fairly common practice for people to abandon children or babies at a hospital entrance, or worse, leave them in gutters or sewer drains along the streets.

So Drex visited the local hospital and was directed to a small crib in a corner in which he found a baby boy the police had found alone on the street. A paper from the hospital said that the tiny boy's name was Jonas.

The sight was absolutely heart-wrenching; Drex could not believe what he saw. Jonas was covered in dirt and lying in his own feces. Flies covered his body and the crib. Jonas made only a small sound, that of a kitten mewing, as he lay on his side, his back arched and his mouth open. Jonas was weak from malnutrition and was also hydrocephalic. It was immediately obvious that Jonas had many, many other physical problems as well.

Drex returned to the Children's Village completely distraught, knowing that Jonas had more medical problems than they could handle, not being a medical facility. Drex told Jo about Jonas and together they prayed about what to do.

They decided to visit a medical clinic in their area at which several American doctors and nurses worked. A pediatrician just happened to be the only doctor that was in the office that day and he wanted to see Jonas immediately. Upon returning to the hospital with the pediatrician, they confirmed that Jonas was in dire need of a shunt in his small head to relieve the fluid that had built up inside. Jonas also had a swollen liver and many other problems that made him too weak to undergo any kind of surgery. Jonas was likely to die in the next two weeks, which wasn't enough time to get him strong enough for surgery.

In Haitian hospitals, parents, family or loved ones are the caregivers who stay with a patient, while the nurses and doctors only provide what little medical care they can. Family or friends have to bring food, purchase any medicine and deliver it to the patient. There was no one for Jonas.

Drex and Jo decided that they couldn't let baby Jonas stay in the hospital to die alone. They returned to the compound and gathered formula, diapers, blankets and other things. Drex went to the police station and signed the papers for Jonas, who became their third little baby.

During their time at the hospital with Jonas, they discovered another place that took in children, located directly across from the hospital, called the Sisters of Charity. The Sisters of Charity is a Catholic organization that houses and cares for children who are starving and dying.

Drex and Jo went and knocked on their gate and told the woman in charge about Jonas, asking her if they could care for him. She immediately said yes, knowing the inhumane condition of the hospital. "We will take him so that he can die like a human," she said.

They continued to visit Jonas over the course of a few weeks and found that while he was clean and well taken care of, he actually got a little better for a few days, before his situation started to deteriorate rapidly. He had a sore on his forehead that had ruptured, leaking spinal fluid, his tiny eyes were not completely open as they were before and his heart rate and breathing were very fast. He was in very critical condition.

For a few weeks, Jonas held on and the nuns at the Sisters of Charity continued to watch over him, keep him clean and love him. Drex and Jo and friends of The Hands and Feet Project visited him regularly and prayed for him daily.

On June 30, 2006, with people all around him, Jonas went to be with the Lord.

Despite the very sad story of Jonas, a blessing came out of meeting and caring for baby Jonas. There are times when, as the Sisters of Charity walk alongside terminally ill or starving babies and children, some of them pull through and live. And some orphans that the Sisters receive are strong and healthy right from the start. Now the Sisters of Charity know about The Hands and Feet Project Children's Village, a place where they can bring those babies and small children to live a normal, healthy and happy life.

Often, when we think about a hope for the future, we immediately turn to the accomplishment of great things. As if "hope" was just another word for "success." Yet when we see the dire needs of some of these orphans and listen to the heartbeat behind The Hands and Feet Project, it becomes clear that for these kids, hope is found in the simple things: having enough food to eat, having clothes to wear, and having the love of another human being who genuinely cares.

For The Hands and Feet Project and for these kids, even though the need is so great and the poverty so overwhelming, there is real hope. This is the fabric of hope, a hope that refuses to see the current devastating circumstances as the end of the story.

Notes

1. "Stats on Haiti," *Unicef.* http://www.unicef.org/media/media_19596.html (accessed May 2, 2006).
2. Donna G. Grigsby, M.D., "Malnutrition," eMedicine. http://www.emedicine.com/ped/topic1360.htm (accessed June 6, 2006).
3. "Stats on Haiti," *Unicef.*
4. Brian D. McLaren, *The Secret Message of Jesus: Uncovering the Truth That Could Change Everything* (Nashville, TN: W Publishing Group, 2006), p. 56.

Chapter 5

BRINGING HEAVEN HERE

Oh, beautiful sound
The joy of heaven here
Oh, wonderful sound
Love of heaven now

"WONDERFUL KING"
DAVID CROWDER BAND

At 9 A.M. on any given Sunday morning, the community
of Cyvadier comes to life. In the cool of the morning air,
women appear with their children, husbands and wives
are out together, and entire families emerge from the surrounding areas, each group walking along the main road
toward the small church. People gather and walk together and there is laughter and conversation about the week.
All these people—families and friends, all of whom are
neighbors to The Hands and Feet Project—make their
way toward the sounds of the local church gathering.

The church in Cyvadier sits only a few hundred yards
away from The Hands and Feet Project property, and it's
clearly visible from the second floor of the main building.
This particular church was founded years ago by a missionary named Tina and several others, and before Drex
and Jo began work on the Children's Village, they often
visited and worked with Tina and this small church community. There are other churches in the area as well, and
although The Hands and Feet Project is not officially tied
to any one of them, this particular church has become a
kind of partner, a kind of spiritual home. Edaline, the
project's first nanny, also attends regularly with her son.

The people of the community come here for a number of reasons. Some come out of duty, while others come
out of true devotion. Some of these people have been
attending this church all their lives, while others are new-
comers to the church and to the faith—and these folks
seem wide-eyed and astonished with each new revelation

from the pastor. Regardless of why they come, as they all enter the long church hall, each one encounters the sounds of community: children laughing and playing, adults talking and sharing stories.

The service is simple, in no way ornate or over-programmed. It begins with singing—lots of singing—and the songs fill the building as people raise their voices in celebration of God. At the front of the church, a man leads the gathering in the song. Along with him, there is a guitar player, a bass player, a pianist and a drummer (most of the time they play in rhythm), all of whom supply the music that brings this little community to life. The centerpiece of this humble ensemble is a homemade drum set fashioned out of wood, leaves and animal skin—reminds one of the simple way of life that most Haitians experience every day.

The feeling given off by this tiny congregation in Cyvadier is one of warmth, grace and welcome. Even in the midst of a culture that is totally different from that of other countries, foreigners are greeted with smiles and made to feel right at home. The main gathering room for the church is approximately 70-feet long and no more than 30-feet wide, although this doesn't include the small classrooms jutting out on each side of the main room. The hall is sparsely decorated, with rows of pews on either side of a main aisle.

There's a saying in Haiti that you can never out-dress a Haitian for church. On most Sundays, this little maxim rings true. No matter how poor the Haitian people are, when it comes time for church, they dress up in their absolute finest. For these churchgoers, church is not simply a location to be visited from week to week. Church is not an institution, a programmatic service, or even a collection of group meetings or events to attend. Church is a community of people gathered around the person of the risen Jesus.

Inside this church today, there is a feeling of *being alive*, a vitality and immediacy that is much different from the feeling on the streets of Jacmel. This church feels different even from the churches across America. This gathering today is more than just a group of people who have the same social calendar that revolves around a list of church activities. In this tiny church, there is a sense that these people place incredible importance and value on their gathering together to celebrate the God in their very midst—these people seem to be tapping directly into this very tangible hope.

You can see it in their eyes and hear it in their voices—these people believe that something is happening in this world. It is not just a hope of eternity someday far away *from* the dirt streets of Cyvadier; it is a hope of something happening in their midst *in* the streets of Cyvadier. They understand that their present situation does not have the final word. God does.

The Joy of Heaven Here

On this particular morning, the little church is packed. Children sit in pews next to their family or friends; some stay still and calm, while others squirm and giggle, generally acting like children do. It is immediately clear that

Local kids smile for the camera at
The Hands and Feet Project site.
There are so many children in the
neighborhood that Drex, Jo and Chris
have thought about setting up a youth
group to minister to all the kids.

these children are a part of the congregation, part of the
main service in which they're expected to participate
from an early age. These children are not just the Church
of tomorrow; they *are* the Church, today.

The congregation sings many songs during the time of
worship, belting out songs of praise and hope never before
heard in an American church. After a lengthy time of
singing, the pastor stands up and speaks to the community. It is common practice to find pastors in Haitian churches who will speak to their congregation for two hours or
more. The pastor of this particular church gives his ser-
mons in Kreyol Ayisyen, or Haitian Creole, which is the
most common language in Haiti, and one of Haiti's official
languages. The other official language is French, which is
spoken by many of the educated Haitians, and most people
have had some exposure to both English and Spanish as well,
due to the country's proximity to the Dominican Republic.

On this day, the pastor of the church stands up front
and opens his arms wide, as if he wants to embrace the
entire community all at once. The words he speaks radi-
ate warmth; his face speaks of acceptance and welcome.

After a few seconds, the pastor says a few words in
Creole, leaving a few of the American-types in the dark,
though Drex and Jo have picked up enough Creole to
understand enough to get by. Some of what is said can be
deduced through the context, and this was the case here.
The congregation responds to these words by picking up
their Bibles. The pastor waits for a moment, as the people

in the congregation find the right place in the text, and then reads the following words from Ephesians:

> But because of his great love for us, God, who is rich in mercy, made us alive with Christ even when we were dead in transgressions—it is by grace you have been saved. And God raised us up with Christ and seated us with him in the heavenly realms in Christ Jesus. For it is by grace you have been saved, through faith—and this not from yourselves, it is the gift of God—not by works, so that no one can boast. For we are God's workmanship, created in Christ Jesus to do good works, which God prepared in advance for us to do (2:4-10).

Reading the same passage in Scripture over and over can sometimes yield new insights each time it is read. In the Jewish tradition, the rabbis used to say that the Scriptures were like a jewel: Hold the jewel up to the light at one angle, and you saw a brilliant spectrum of color; turn it another way, and you saw another. The jewel never changed, and neither did the light. What brought forth the brilliant colors was something mysterious, perhaps even living. In a similar way, God is somehow always speaking through Scripture, always revealing deeper shades of what is real and true through the pages of the text.

Here in this small church in Cyvadier, sitting next to these beautiful Haitian orphan children, reading this verse declares incredible power. In this foreign land, it is as if someone has turned the jewel just slightly and uncovered a new understanding of the power of this passage of Scripture. The mystery of the Ephesians passage is that we've not only been saved *from* condemnation, but that we've also been saved by grace *to* or *for* something.

Understanding that we have been invited to be a part of this greater Kingdom movement is central to the Christian faith. This is why it is essential for those who follow Jesus, in every part of the world, to stand up on behalf of the widows and the orphans, the marginalized, and the oppressed; to act to change issues of poverty and injustice. We need to be involved with these things not because they make us better people, but because God's desire is for us to help *transform* this world. His desire is for us to partner with Him to align this world with the way He intended for it to operate. We are partners with God in the restoration and reconciliation of all things (see 2 Cor. 5:17-19). We have been invited to bring the light of God to a world that is filled with darkness, despair and brokenness.

This is the message that the people in a little church in Cyvadier hear on this day. It is a humbling word that speaks to the entire Church, the larger Body of Christ. The joy in the eyes of the people in that church is a reminder of this, a reminder of that feeling that as Christians, we are a part of something so much bigger than ourselves—something much bigger even that the problems and strains and hardships sitting under the roof of this little church.

A typical street scene in the community of Jacmel. The city is home to
approximately 15,000 people.

These Haitian Christians believe that they are part of a revolutionary movement that is occurring in this world and that they are part of a community that is experiencing the kingdom of God in a very real way. It has changed them, and they want it to change the world around them.

And so, they gather together to sing, to pray, to remind one another that this is not all there is.

A Slice of Heaven

The service comes to a close, and as it does so, everyone stands for the final prayer and benediction. Near the back row, a little girl with pigtails and a purple dress stands up and clutches tight to her mother. She is about four years old and her eyes sparkle as she looks around the hall. As the pastor prepares for the benediction, she looks across the aisle with her big, beautiful brown eyes and smiles wide, her face a picture of innocence.

One can't help but wonder what the future will hold for her. What kind of life will she have? Will she have enough food to eat? Will she have enough clothes to wear? What about all the things she doesn't have? Will she become just another statistic? Where is the hope?

Then the pastor reads the words of the benediction from Matthew 6:9-10 over the congregation:

Our Father in heaven,
hallowed be your name,
your kingdom come,

your will be done
on earth as it is in heaven.

The pastor dismisses the people and, once again, the sound of laughter fills the little church. People hug each other, smile, shake hands and kiss the cheeks of their neighbors. Kids start to play again, finally released from sitting quietly in the church pews all morning.

The midday sun shines bright and hot in Haiti today, forcing everyone to squint as they exit the building, hands perched over the ridge of their brows. The sun illuminates the land then, as people file outside, the greens of the grasses bursting with color, while the deep, rich browns of the earth contrast greatly against the blue of the sky. And the hope and joy of the people seems to spread through the land as they walk out into the streets.

Through the faith of these Haitian Christians, and the faith of other Christians throughout this land, it is evident that Jesus is alive and at work in Haiti. Jesus is working inside the people here and they understand that they are part of a greater movement. They understand that they are part of the Body of Christ around the world, and that they can help.

For these Christians who laugh and sing with such overflowing hope, the Kingdom has come near.

And for a short time, it feels like a slice of heaven.

Chapter 6

GREATER THINGS

Very truly I tell you, all who have faith in me will do the works I have been doing, and they will do even greater things than these, because I am going to the Father

John 14:12

While it is sometimes said that there are more missionaries in Haiti than almost anywhere else, and even though a majority of the population are professing Catholics or Protestants (despite the wide influences of vodou), the people of Haiti are still in dire economic need. The missionaries who have come down have preached the good news and have succeeded in planting the gospel into the soil, but people still find it difficult to feed, clothe and shelter their own families. The need in this country is overwhelming and it is immediate.

"There still aren't enough missionaries yet," says Chris Cotton. "The people here are all still only eating one meal a day. I think that's one reason we are not linked to any denomination or specific church—because of the hoops you have to jump through—we are instead supported by all sorts of denominations and groups, and this has allowed us to move very quickly."

What can one small organization do to help? Is it even possible to operate in the face of such overwhelming hunger and poverty?

Entering into the Solution

There's this fascinating story about Jesus. In the time of Jesus, all rabbis would send their disciples out into the world on their own to test what they had learned. The disciples went out with the rabbi's authority to put into practice what they had seen their rabbi doing. In Mark 6:30-31, Jesus' disciples had just come back from such an experience:

The apostles gathered around Jesus and reported to him all they had done and taught. Then, because so many people were coming and going that they did not even have a chance to eat, he said to them, "Come with me by yourselves to a quiet place and get some rest."

The disciples were filled with excitement and energy. They couldn't wait to tell Jesus all that they had accomplished in His name. But something larger was about to occur—something beautiful and mysterious.

So they went away by themselves in a boat to a solitary place. But many who saw them leaving recognized them and ran on foot from all the towns and got there ahead of them. When Jesus landed and saw a large crowd, he had compassion on them, because they were like sheep without a shepherd. So he began teaching them many things.

   By this time it was late in the day, so his disciples came to him. "This is a remote place," they said, "and it's already very late. Send the people away so that they can go to the surrounding countryside and villages and buy themselves something to eat" (vv. 32-35).

Jesus took His disciples away to get some needed rest, but the crowds relentlessly pursued Christ. The people met them on the shore before Jesus and the disciples even had a chance to step off the boat. The disciples, sensing that the day was coming to a close, approached Jesus with a practical problem: There were a lot of people here, and it was getting late. What should they do about food for all the people?

> He answered, "You give them something to eat." They said to him, "That would take almost a year's wages! Are we to go and spend that much on bread and give it to them to eat?" (v. 37).

Rather than giving them an easy answer, Jesus took the conversation to a whole different level: "You give them something to eat." Jesus turned the conversation back on them, in essence asking them, "What are you going to do about it?"

The disciples' response was classic: "Are you kidding, Jesus? You want us to do *what*? Are you crazy? Do you even *know* what you're asking?" The problem was just too big for them. There was no way that they had the resources to feed the people in the crowd. But Jesus had the disciples just where He wanted them: They saw the need. They realized their inadequacy to meet the need all on their own. The situation seemed impossible.

> "How many loaves do you have?" he asked. "Go and see." When they found out, they said, "Five—

and two fish." Then Jesus directed them to have all the people sit down in groups on the green grass. So they sat down in groups of hundreds and fifties. Taking the five loaves and the two fish and looking up to heaven, he gave thanks and broke the loaves. Then he gave them to his disciples to set before the people. He also divided the two fish among them all. They ate and were satisfied, and the disciples picked up twelve basketfuls of broken pieces of bread and fish. The number of the men who had eaten was five thousand (vv. 38-44).

Like all good rabbis, Jesus answered a question with another question. He took the conversation to a whole new level. This was bigger than just feeding the people who had come to listen; Jesus was trying to open the disciples' eyes to the solution that was right in their midst.

How many loaves do you have? It's as if Jesus was saying, "Let's not start with what you don't have; let's start with what you do have." Even as the sun was setting, the light was beginning to dawn.

Five loaves—and two fish.

In the hands of Jesus, even five loaves and two fish were more than enough. Perhaps this is part of the Kingdom message. The miracles of Jesus are more than just shows of power; they are demonstrations of the possibilities of the kingdom of God. When the kingdom of God has come, what we think is impossible is suddenly transformed into the possible.

What the disciples learned that day near the shore of the Sea of Galilee has implications for us as well. In a mysterious sort of way, we are being invited into the solution.

We are being invited into that solution for our world, from the streets of our own neighborhoods to the slums of Haiti. We get to be partners with God in the healing and mending of this world. Our role is not to stand by and watch, simply praying for God to do something, although that is important. It is for us to enter into the solution as an active participant. Rather than being blinded by what we can't do, we need to awaken to all that we can do through Him.

The lesson in this story from Mark 6 shows that it is not about what we bring, but to whom we have brought it. We are partners with God in the healing and mending of the world. Our role is to bring what we can, undeterred by what appears impossible, because with Jesus, all the rules have changed.

Being the Hands and Feet of Jesus

Jesus says something pretty staggering in John 14:12: "Very truly I tell you, all who have faith in me will do the works I have been doing, and they will do even greater things than these, because I am going to the Father."

Why is this staggering? Well, Jesus seems like a hard act to follow. But there's a little more going on here that

A worker puts the finishing touches on the porch of The Hands and Feet building.

many readers notice. Sometimes in our rush to dive into the second half of the verse, we forget that Jesus says something equally astounding in the first half.

He says, "All who have faith in me will do the works that I have been doing."

Jesus makes an enormous assumption here. Those who are His followers should be doing the things that He is doing. Apparently in Jesus' mind it is impossible to call yourself a follower and not have your life look like the person you are following. To be a disciple in the first century meant that you had committed your life to following your rabbi, to having your life look like his. It was not enough to simply talk like your rabbi. It was not enough to look like your rabbi. It wasn't even enough to be able to teach like your rabbi.

The goal of a first-century *talmidim*, or disciple, was to do what your rabbi did.[1] If you were a disciple, your life looked like his. The things he did, you did. The things that he was about, you were about. The things that were closest to his heart were the things that were closest to yours.

So for Jesus, this is nonnegotiable. If you are His follower, then your life must look like His. If you are His follower, you will listen to, absorb and orient your life around His teachings and way of life. If you are not trying to live the way of Jesus, then perhaps you are not His follower. Jesus said as much.

Now what about all these greater things that Jesus talked about? Is Jesus actually serious that we would do greater things than He did? How is this possible?

What He was inviting the disciples into was to be involved in doing something greater, something more expansive. Through His death and resurrection, Jesus opened the door wide for the kingdom of God to break into the world and invade the earth.

So His was a call to do greater things, and it was an invitation the disciples could not refuse.

The Hands and Feet Project is just one of many expressions of the kingdom of God breaking into this world. It is just one expression of the "greater things" that Jesus talked about, one expression of trying to be obedient to the things that are closest to the heart of Jesus. It is an expression of love and of caring for those in need who otherwise would have little hope in this world.

If you were to ask Chris Cotton, he would see the larger picture like this: "Love transcends all cultures. This Project is about bringing love and hope to the orphans of Haiti. They need to be loved and cared for, and we believe that it is the responsibility of Christians to be out there doing it. It's not that we are doing anything better than anyone else; we've just found a small section of Haiti where we can spread the good news of the kingdom of God.

"What I'd love is to see a revolution in Christianity—to see it break out of the chains of cultural, compartmental Christianity and once again be filled with passion and compassion. It means a change in how we see our resources and what we see as the mission of the Church.

It will change how we see everything.

"We as the Church need to realize that we are supposed to be a part of the solution. God is not calling us to sit in a church building and pray that something might happen. He wants us to get out of the building and personally do something about the needs. As the people of God, we desperately need to *re-imagine* how we can mobilize our faith. We need to learn how to serve those around us and those in need. It is about putting ourselves out there and letting God show us where we need to be.

"It may sound trite, but it's profoundly true: As Christians, we are the hands and feet of Jesus. We need to live what the Scriptures tell us to do—to love the least and the helpless, to do something about rampant poverty in this world. How many verses are there about taking care of those who are poor? How many verses are there about standing up for justice in this world? Poverty is a moral issue."

Much like the disciples, it would be easy for us to stand on the side of the impossible. It would be easy to see the needs and be overwhelmed with all that we are not able to do. But if anything is clear from the life of Jesus, it is this: The world of the impossible has been overthrown, and in its place a Kingdom of possibilities has invaded.

The Kingdom has come near.

The mystery that we have been invited into is the same mystery that the disciples were confronted with on the shore of the Sea of Galilee. We are not Kingdom spectators in this world. In fact, we are active participants, partnering with God in the transformation of peoples lives. More than just talking about what needs to be done—or even merely praying for it to happen—we are invited to embody the answer to a broken and hurting world.

As a wise man said once, "Be the change you want to see in the world."[2]

To do anything less would be, well, anti-Jesus.

So how many loaves do you have? Go and see.

Notes

1. For a much fuller treatment of the subject of first-century rabbis and their *talmidim* and the implications for today, read "Dust," the fifth chapter of Rob Bell's book *Velvet Elvis* (Grand Rapids, MI: Zondervan, 2005).

2. Mahatma Ghandi (1869-1948), the great Indian philosopher and humanitarian, as quoted at http://en.thinkexist.com/quotation/be_the_change_you_want_to_see_in_the_world/148490.html (accessed May 7, 2006).

Chapter 7
A LOOK BACK

I'm alive
The moment I let go brought passion to my soul
I'm alive
My heart's been rearranged and will
never be the same

"I'm Alive"
Audio Adrenaline

Cyvadier has the most amazing beaches. Unlike the kind of beaches that have cold, murky water, these beaches have the vibrant blue water that you see on the Travel Channel. They are warm and inviting, just like the people of Cyvadier.

When you see the ocean and listen to the waves, you are reminded once again that in the midst of great poverty—in the midst of great despair—you are still on a Caribbean island. It's truly ironic, really.

The sun has set for the evening and the cool offshore breeze has come in. Mark, Will and the team drive down a gravel road, park Drex and Jo's pickup, and head off down by the water. The destination: a beautiful restaurant set off from the main gravel road with this absolutely amazing view of the ocean.

Sitting at a table by the railing, our meals arrive: four different kinds of fresh fish. As the meal is savored, so is the conversation. There is laughter. There are stories of the early days of Audio Adrenaline, when the guys were in Bible college and used to drive from town to town staying in host homes. Some of the places they stayed were amazing, while others were . . . well, that's another story.

One time, the band was on the road and came to the church that they were supposed to play in that night. The only problem was that the people in the church thought that they were getting a vocal ensemble from the Bible college. When the band started unloading their gear—like the amps and drums—the people were shocked, to say the least. Satan had entered the building!

Another time, the band came to play at what they thought was going to be a church, but which actually turned out to be six people at a picnic table. "Man, those are amazing memories," says Mark, closing his eyes as if transporting himself back to those earlier days, "ones that we'll never forget. We loved those days. That is what it's all about."

As we sit around the table, the conversation soon turns to the events of the past few days: the people of Cyvadier we've met, Thamara and Jabez, the YWAM missionaries that we ran into on a half-day excursion cliff-diving into deep water about an hour away from the Project.

After the plates are cleared and everyone is thoroughly enjoying the moment, the coffee arrives. Will, the band's official coffee connoisseur, takes the first sip and pronounces his judgment. "This coffee is flat-out amazing," he says. "This is the best coffee in the world. It's hot though. I think my innards are on fire."

The ocean breeze is cool, slowly moving the branches of the palm trees that stand between the table and the ocean. In the not-too-far distance, you can hear the undulation and crashing of the waves on the beach shore. Everyone is in a reflective mood. The conversation flows.

Mark: When I think about this place, I think about the stories of people. One story in particular really had an impact on us and encouraged us to think about building an orphanage. Tina Eisenhower is this missionary friend of ours here in Haiti that my dad was working with. Over about a 10-year period, as my parents were coming here on and off, they would help her with her electrical system and solar panels and help keep her truck up and running. She would always tell my parents, "I'm never going to adopt a Haitian. I'm never going to do that."

One day, Tina was brought this little baby named Rachel, who was the daughter of a woman who was really into vodou. Rachel's mother had already had several of her children die due to the fact that she would go on these drinking binges and basically neglect them. One child starved to death; another was literally swept out to sea while the mother was partying on the beach with a group of people. On one of her binges—which often lasted for days on end—she left Rachel alone in their little shack. Days went on, and the baby got hungry. She ended up eating whatever was loose on the floor, in the dirt and mud.

She was found and brought to Tina, who took her to the doctor. The doctor said that Rachel was going to die—there was no hope for her. Suddenly, Tina had this sense from God that she was supposed to take this sick little girl in. The doctor told her that she was wasting her time on this little girl—there was no way that the baby was going to survive. Tina pleaded with the doctor. Finally, he gave in and showed her how to do an IV on Rachel. The doctor wouldn't even do it himself; he just told Tina how to do it and told her to go home. To him, Rachel and Tina were just a waste of time.

Will McGinnis visits The Hands
and Feet Children's Village in
the summer of 2006.

So Tina took the baby home and took care of her, giving her the IV and just holding her, loving on her. Eventually, Rachel started getting better. It's really a miracle if you think about it. Tina had never planned on having a Haitian child in her home in the first place. And then to think that she loved and cared for Rachel, literally bringing her back from the dead. Rachel is 10 or maybe 12 years old now. She is vibrant and alive, and so smart. She's still with Tina to this day. In fact, she goes to school right down the road here.

I know that story really affected Bob and me. We were just blown away at how much a child can develop and grow into this incredible, vibrant, loving person if he or she has a great home, a great situation to grow up in, a great environment with great parents and a Christian family. That's what The Hands and Feet Project is all about. What's incredible is that Rachel's story is not unique. In fact, it's all too common among the orphans here. If no one were here to take care of them, they'd be caught in a very bad situation. This is the story of so many of these kids, and their story needs to be told.

Haiti has the most missionaries per capita on the planet, and I think there is a good reason for that. The needs are immense. Every day, children die or are put into slavery. Haiti is not a country with a lot of social programs. There is literally nothing here. There is nowhere to turn, no help whatsoever. No welfare system, no social medicine and, unless there are mission organizations or orphanages that give these children support and take them in, the situation just continues on. So the need here is great. It's beyond the issue of mere evangelism—it's about taking care of kids for the sake of taking care of kids, because that is what Jesus would want us to do. To take these kids in and give them the opportunity to just live, and even to know Jesus, it is just a miracle for these kids.

Will: I think it's important for people to know that while the need here can seem so great—almost as if you could never make a difference—to do nothing is perhaps even worse. Even if it's just one person that you touch, it is worth all the time and effort. That should be your goal: to just touch one person and not be overwhelmed by the larger picture. Touching one life is worth it all. It really is.

Mark: I think about Thamara, our first little orphan in the Project. When we got her, she had giardia and worms. She was malnourished. In fact, at two years old she couldn't stand up or even hold her head up. When you held her, it was like holding a rag doll.

Her mother had major complications and a stroke during childbirth. It took almost a year for her mother to die. During that year, her mother was unable to care for Thamara, so she was in really bad health for the first year of her life. Tina knew about the situation, and told us that what was desperately needed down here to take care of all these kids was an orphanage. She had kids brought to her every week. They just kept bringing them to her and asking for help. So Tina was pretty instrumental in bringing the project here to Cyvadier.

It's amazing, really. The area of Jacmel is one of the nicest parts of Haiti. It is still very poor, but in about a 10-mile radius there are probably 100 orphans or more living in poverty like you can't imagine. As followers of Jesus, we need to do something.

Hands and Feet (HAF): That reminds me of the passage in James 1:27. As followers of Jesus, we must do something. If you want to please God, it's not about rules, but about justice. It's about being about what Jesus would be about.

Mark: I think the whole context of that verse is that merely being religious is unattainable. It's like James is showing us what some think religion is all about, and we see that there is no way we could live that way. Then he moves into showing what true religion is all about. Religion in its truest form is when we reach out to the people around us. It's not about us trying to be good merely for the sake of being perfect or being sinless. True religion is when we look after the less fortunate. James basically states, "Yeah, there's no way we can attain this, but you can do this: Look after the needy." I think that is when the Church becomes what it should be. If the Church tries to be the Church in any other way, it falls drastically short.

Will: It reminds me of what Micah 6:8 says: "What does the LORD require of you? To act justly and to love mercy and to walk humbly with your God." It's mind boggling what we can get caught up in trying to be religious. We think it's all about the rules, especially about what we shouldn't do: *Don't do this. Don't do that.* But what about the things we *should* do? It's as if God is trying to tell us, "I don't want your external show of religion. I want you. I want your heart." Only when God truly has us and our heart will we actually understand what God wants, and that will motivate us to look after the least of these. I just think that we fill our lives with so many things that we are blinded from even seeing the least of these, let alone doing anything about it.

Mark: When you come here, you start thinking less of yourself, and then God opens your eyes. You see the least of these and are forced to consider what you're going to do about it. When you come to a place like Haiti, you are not bombarded with things that make you think selfishly. Your whole mind-set changes.

I think it's foolish not to be involved in giving yourself away, because when you read James 1:27, you realize that it is not about you. It's about investing in others, and in doing that you get closer to God. Becoming Jesus' hands and feet, it puts you out there. It strips away your preconceived ideas of what is important in life. It shows you what is really real.

Will: I've had people tell me that to change your attitude, you need to start living the attitude you want to have. It's so true. To change your heart, you need to jump in and do something that will stretch your heart.

Mark: I think a lot of it has to do with the noise of our lives. It's pretty obvious that most of us live at a crazy, frenetic pace. We've got television, e-mail, cell phones. But when you come here and don't have any of those things, you begin to realize that you truly don't need them. You begin to realize how much of your life has been stolen by the pace at which you live your life. You come here and life is just different. It's a richer existence.

HAF: The richness and depth of life that you get from being involved in a project such as Hands and Feet is incredible. If you let these opportunities pass you by because you're too busy, you're cheating yourself out of hearing God in ways that are profound and rich.

Will: The gospel says that it will dumbfound the wise and be simple to a child. I think children get it because they haven't had the time to get busy or to learn to be selfish. Life is a joy. Life is about exploration. The wise man tries to figure it out, but the child just enjoys it. The song "Good Life" keeps popping in my head. We wrote that song about tasting the good life, which is when you give up all that you're striving for. When you

Chris Cotton, executive director of The Hands and Feet Project, with a local friend.

give your life away, you find it in God.

Mark: The chorus is, "This is the good life, I lost everything I could ever want or dream of. This is the good life, 'cause I found everything I could ever want here in Your arms." It's like when it appears that someone has hit rock bottom. Rather than those times being moments of despair, perhaps those are the moments when you are closest to God, more than you ever really imagined. In those moments, life gets richer and more beautiful, more colorful and passionate. The same thing can happen here. When you give your life away, you get something greater and richer than you could ever imagine.

A while ago I was reading *The Utmost for His Highest*, and I was really hit by something I read: If you don't take your boat and release yourself from the dock, invariably God will send a storm to knock you off the moorings. God's desire is that we get out into the open water, because it is there that the real relationship happens. A real relationship with God doesn't happen in the harbor, safely tied up to the dock. The boat wasn't made to stay tied to the dock; it was meant to sail in the open water.

This is where the decision comes in. Are you going to unleash the boat and go out into the open water, or are you going to stay where it is safe and predictable? You can choose to go yourself, or God will take you there—either way, you are going out there. Choosing to serve is a great way to get out into the open water. It's a great way to learn to rely on God and have your eyes opened. Getting out into the open water gets you out of what is predictable and out of your self-centeredness.

Will: I think that is what we're dealing with as a band. Are we going to fully rely on God for the next chapter of our lives? I was thinking about what Mark said, that my kids are probably going to have to see this project through. It's made me ask, "Can I make that commitment for them?" It's pretty overwhelming. When you try to wrap your mind around what the future holds for The Hands and Feet Project, the truth is that we don't know what lies ahead. We have to rely on God—that He knows and is going to put the people in place to carry this thing forward into the future. You just have to let go and rely on Him, which is how the Project has gotten this far and this fast anyway.

HAF: Speaking of the future, when you close your eyes and try to look 5, perhaps 10 years down the line for The Hands and Feet Project, what do you see?

Mark: I tell you, I have all kinds of crazy ideas. First of all, I'd love to see 50 or 60 kids in the orphanage. I would like to see a place that's really beautiful. Not beautiful in a sense of having nice buildings, but a beauty and a joy that comes from the kids and the people who work there. I see groups coming from the United States ministering to the orphans and being ministered to by the orphans, because I think that happens more than the opposite. I see a food program that connects with the community as a whole, with medical treatments given on the campus of the Project.

I have a real passion for the youth of the community as well, because so many of them are not really tied into a church. Take Jonesy, who lives next door to the Project. He went to church with us this morning because I begged him to go—that was cool. I'd love to start a youth group, a place for kids to come and worship the Lord and explore what it means to have a real, intimate relationship with God.

So I guess my overall desire is to see these kids grow up in a healthy environment, but also to transform the greater community with medical assistance and a food program. We talked about doing a church plant up in the mountains at some point, but that might be further down the road.

Then, on a much larger scale, I would love to see The Hands and Feet Project plant orphanages in other parts of the world in partnership with other Christian musicians. It would be great to find artists who have a passion for this kind of ministry in other countries, wherever they feel God is leading them into—like Ecuador, or Guatemala, or Romania. It would be amazing to come alongside other artists and make that dream a reality by helping them with leadership or raising the finances to make it happen. It would be great to take the two things that we are really passionate about, music and missions, and combine them to see what can happen. It would be amazing to mix those two things up to create something really miraculous.

Will: What's ironic about our organization is that everything we have done for almost 20 years now—ever since Mark and I met, really—has been done flying by the seat of our pants. This one thing, The Hands and Feet Project, is one of the first things we've done in which we've actually sat down and planned how to make it happen.

Mark: With music, it is so different. Making music is intangible, unpredictable. You make a record, and you never know what's going to happen. You can't really plan for it. This project is like that in some ways, but very different in others. This is not about us being creative. It's about us doing the work. It's about concrete action. And that has been great fun.

Will: I think that when you get into the music industry, your dreams are about selling a million records, or having a gold record, or getting on this tour or that tour. But I think you have to ask the hard questions: *What's your real motivation? Why do you want those things? Is it about money? Is it about fame?* I think the reality is that it is stupid to base your life around all of those things. What is important is to base your life around what God wants, which may be very different. I think that what we are doing with this project is going to be the most important thing for us.

It's about dreaming something bigger than ourselves, outside of ourselves. All the fame and notoriety will fade away, but the things you invest in that are larger than yourself—those are the things that will remain.

Mark: You can sit here today and think, *This is what is going to happen.* But will it really? When we were in college, if someone had told us that we were going to have the career we have had, we would have told them that they were insane. We just thought that was never possible. I think that one thing we've learned over the years is that God can do anything. It's as if God were saying, "Come on, take a risk. Come out here in the open water and see what I can do." That's what we've been doing for years. It's the story of Audio. It's also the story of Hands and Feet.

HAF: With the Audio side of life beginning to wind down, it seems as if one chapter in your lives is ending and another is beginning. How do you see the two working together?

Mark: I don't even know if I consider them together. I know that one helps the other, but they're different. Hands and Feet will be around long after Audio Adrenaline.

Will: I know that for me, there have been times when I have seriously wondered if it was a good idea to end Audio Adrenaline, for the sake of using it to help The Hands and

Feet Project. Then again, maybe that's like putting God back in the box again. I don't really know at this point. My pastor and I have been talking lately about going from glory to glory—that everything we do is a preparation for the next thing we're going to do. It's like the idea of the wineskins. God never wants to give you an old wineskin to put new wine in. He wants to give you a new wineskin to put new wine in. There is a time to let go of the past.

Those are some of the things that I have been dwelling on lately. All I know is that somehow we started this project here, and we'll be darned if we're going to let it go down. We believe that God is going to sustain it, even without us. I think that if we fell off the earth tomorrow, He would still sustain it. It's not about us. It's about what God is doing here.

I believe that God gave us the credibility through Audio Adrenaline to start something like this and promote it. People knew who we were and what we stood for. They knew that we loved the Church and loved the kids in the youth group, even when it wasn't cool to be about the youth group. Without even knowing it, that was the preparation for what we are doing here. Now we can encourage young people to come to Haiti because we have that relationship with youth pastors and youth groups.

So the credibility that we have with the Church has helped The Hands and Feet Project. As far as the legacy of the Project goes, I think it has a bright future. I truly believe that there is no greater legacy you can leave than to do something way bigger than yourself. Legacy is not about making a name for yourself. It's about reaching out to others, especially the least of those.

Even if people forget your name, it really doesn't matter. It's not about promoting yourself. It's about living the course that God set out for you. You can't promote yourself in God's economy—you just end up getting in the way or someplace else where He didn't want you in the first place. I'm captivated by the idea that we could leave a legacy of this project that could inspire a whole country to change.

HAF: I like what you said about questioning the decision to keep Audio around in order to help The Hands and Feet Project. It says that this project is the central issue and that Audio is just this dispensable thing toward some other greater goal.

Will: It's been like that for a few years now, honestly.

Mark: I think that what Audio was able to do was really, really special, because it allowed us to reach a multitude of people that potentially could do what we're doing here. But I think that we are becoming smaller and smaller while this is getting bigger and bigger. That is what has been getting me excited lately. I mean, I'm tired of just telling people to go do something great. I want to do it myself. I personally want to be involved in a vehicle that is making a difference, and this is. It may be a smaller vehicle, but the effect it can have on 100 orphans is amazing. I want to do it and do it well.

Will: Back when we started Audio, we were all about summer camps. They were great. We were able to dig into those kids' lives for a week. We knew everything about them—their hurts, their fears and their dreams. We cried with them. We prayed with them. We even saw a lot of them come to the Lord. Real impact is in the relationships. It's not when you're in a band that flies in, does a show, and then flies out. You don't really get to see any of the fruit. It's like Mark said, smaller is often better. It's about the relationships. Those are the things that are going to last.

HAF: You really want to affect change in this country, not just be an inch deep and a mile wide. That's very counter-culture—even counter-Christian culture. Too many people want to be larger than life or make a name for themselves. I think this orphanage is a very different expression of what Audio is all about, and one that will not go away.

Will: I think that is so true. I want my wife and kids to start thinking on that level. It's not about the name you make for yourself but about what you do to change this world in small ways—one life at a time.

HAF: Mark, on the flight from Miami you talked about the "great descent." What is that, and what does it mean for you?

Mark: The great descent is when people reach a point in their lives where their priorities finally become adjusted to the truth. It's the point when you turn away from trying to be successful and putting away treasures here on Earth—the things that you are fighting for that don't matter that much.

Usually, something happens that shakes your world. You realize what is important and you give up trying to reach some pinnacle of worldly success. Your vision and perspective begin to change, and you get more clarity. You begin a great descent. You might start to decline in wealth or prestige or any number of things. At the same time, your life becomes richer. Instead of shallowness, you find an amazing depth there.

I feel as if I'm starting my great descent. Not because I've reached some pinnacle of wisdom or fame; it's just a sense of a turning point of what's important to me. You have to embrace the descent and let it go. The things that are smaller become more important, and instead of being an inch deep and a mile wide, you're an inch wide and a mile deep. I think the same thing is happening to Audio Adrenaline. I think Audio is on that great descent. We see this project as one of the most important things that we'll ever do in our whole lives, including Audio Adrenaline. This project is not about doing massive, unbelievable, amazing things. It's about having amazing relationships right here and affecting a small group of people. It might not be miraculous if you read about it in a book or saw the numbers of people who were affected by it. But it is doing something beautifully profound. That's why I think it's foolish not to be involved in something like this.

Hopefully, this book isn't just read by kids. I think that what's happened in this conversation and in our minds—and is still happening in our hearts—is almost more for people who are doing a second chapter in their lives or are beginning the second chapter. What we are learning is this: Don't just rest and ride out the rest of life, but go deeper and farther out into the open waters. I hope this book will encourage people to do just that.

Will: As Audio has been in this great descent, the shows have become way more important. They're richer. We try to grasp every second of them. Before, we were so busy that it felt like we went in, did the show and were out again. I think the shows have become more enjoyable now. We're in such a better place. We just want to enjoy ourselves onstage and enjoy being with people.

I think what Mark said is so important. When you are going through the great descent, it's not about climbing some mountain. You are no longer consumed with what you are doing as much as who you are becoming. It's not about fame or notoriety. It's about the impact you make on a life.

Mark: You can try to do great things for God yet still miss the point. Is it about you? Or is it about God? When I come here, I see things more clearly. I can come here and lay blocks, mix concrete or play with the kids, and I literally become the hands and feet of Jesus. I forget about building my empire in the United States. I know that sounds kind of crazy, but that's what I really feel. Back home I'm always busy going here, going there, going to the office, going to do a show or coming home from one. It feels as if it is all about achieving something or becoming someone.

But when I come here, it's different. My stress and selfishness melt away. I'm more aware of people, things, needs, wants, hurts, pains and happiness. When I'm here, I feel more alive than ever before.

I'm just . . . alive.

Chapter 8

USE YOUR HANDS
AND FEET

GET INVOLVED WITH
THE HANDS AND FEET PROJECT

Did you read the book and find yourself wanting to get involved? Did you feel compelled to help the children of Haiti through The Hands and Feet Project? The following short section lists a number of specific ways you can get involved in the project and help orphans in Haiti right now. Read through the list and take action. Here's how you can step up and use your hands and feet:

Pray for the Project
- Pray for protection of the individuals traveling to and from Haiti each year to work with the HAF project.
- Pray for bold and courageous leadership, and specifically for Drex and Jo Stuart.
- Pray for wisdom in continuing to build more housing for the Children's Village.
- Pray for donors to help support the ministry financially.
- Pray about your potential involvement with the project.

Support The Hands and Feet Project Financially
- Tax-deductible gifts must be made out to "Hands and Feet Project" and sent to:

The Hands and Feet Project
P.O. Box 682105
Franklin, TN 37068-2105

· You may also make a gift through the online donation
page on the HAF website (www.hafproject.org).

Tell People About the Project
· Seek out leaders in your church and community
and let them know why you are excited about this
project.
· Tell your friends and family about this book.
· Tell others to visit the website and consider how they
might be able to get involved (www.hafproject.org).

Go to the Website (www.hafproject.org)
· Read about the project and see photos and video
of the kids in Cyvadier, Haiti.
· Raise your general awareness of the economic and politi-
cal situation in Haiti.
· Link to The Hands and Feet Project on Myspace.com.
· Sign up to receive project updates on
www.hafproject.org.

Contact the Hands and Feet Project
· Mark Stuart and Will McGinnis are available to come to
churches or youth groups to present the work of The
Hands and Feet Project in Cyvadier, Haiti.

· Send your encouraging letters to Mark, Will, Chris, Drex and Jo at the address below.

The Hands and Feet Project
P.O. Box 682105
Franklin, TN 37068-2105
www.hafproject.org
(615) 300-7497
info@hafproject.org

A DEEPER DIALOGUE

The following questions are offered as discussion starters, either for the individual reader or a small group that is working through the book together. Although these questions are a beginning point, they are not the only questions that can help explore the thoughts presented in this book. Our desire is that they will help lead you to better, more personal questions.

Sometimes the best questions do not lead to quick and easy answers but raise a whole set of other questions. Questions should not lead merely to answers but to a transformation of the questioner. Bono, the lead singer of U2, put it this way: "Being a Christian hasn't given me all the answers; instead it's given me a whole new set of questions."[1]

If you are reading this book as a part of a study group, it may be beneficial to begin your time by allowing each person to share the story of their spiritual journey. This will help you get to know one another better as well as help others understand and appreciate the perspective of where each person is coming from.

May this experience make you ask deeper and more penetrating questions of what it might mean to be a follower of Jesus in this world.

Welcome to the journey.

Note

1. Tony Campolo, *Speaking My Mind: The Radical Evangelical Prophet Tackles the Tough Issues Christians Are Afraid to Face* (Nashville, TN: W Publishing Group, 2004), p. xii.

CHAPTER 1: FLIGHT TO HAITI

1. As you read the first chapter of the book, what connected with you? Was there anything that stood out or that you disagreed with?

2. How do you see the following quote from the chapter to be true:

   We essentially live in a God-drenched world. Therefore, central to what it means to be a Christian is the belief that God is alive and in every moment, in every place.

   What are some of the implications for how we view and live life?

3. Read Exodus 24:12. Think about the words and what God is communicating to Moses. What are the areas in your life in which you need to slow down and live fully present? What are the places in your life that you desperately need to hear God say, "Come up, and be, exist, awaken, rest, breathe"?

4. Read James 1:27 and Micah 6:8. What's so revolutionary about these verses? What are the writers trying to get across? Take a few moments and rewrite the verses in your own words.

5. Take some time to explore the following Scriptures: Leviticus 19:9-10; Deuteronomy 24:17-18; Isaiah 1:16-17; Jeremiah 5:26-29; Ezekiel 16:49-50; and Matthew

25:31-46. What is the message of these passages?

Going Deeper: Before your next group meeting, each person should pick one of the websites listed in the resource section to explore. Find out what the organization or the website is all about. What does it teach you about Haiti? At your next meeting, share a little about what you found.

CHAPTER 2: THE SOUNDS OF HOPE

1. What spoke to you as you read the chapter? What surprised you about Haiti? What burdened you about Haiti?
2. What are some words that you would use to describe Haiti's historical or political journey?
3. What website did you visit for the Going Deeper section in chapter 1? What did you find as you explored that website? What surprised you or challenged you?
4. Do you think God cares about the political landscape of a country? If so, why?
5. In what areas do you see Haiti needing hope?
6. What could bring hope to Haiti?

Going Deeper: Before your next group meeting, each person should spend an hour on the Internet exploring the issue of poverty. Using Google or some other search engine, have each person do a search using some combination of terms such as "poverty," "Haiti," "orphans," "social justice," "economics," "kingdom of God," "debt relief," "Christianity," or some other term that comes to mind. Spend a few minutes searching various websites to learn more about issues of poverty and social justice, looking specifically at what your responsibility should be as a follower of Jesus. Be sure to bring any interesting articles you may find with you to the group meeting.

CHAPTER 3: FROM THE PORCH

1. Is there anything that Mark or Will said in this interview that had an impact on you? If so, what was it?

2. What did you learn from your research on the Internet about poverty and social justice? What is the Church doing about it? What should the Church be doing about it?

3. In this chapter, Mark states, "How amazing would it be to look back on the AIDS crisis and what's happened in these Third World countries and be able to say that these are the people that came to the rescue, these followers of Jesus? It would be incredible—the Church doing and being what the Church is supposed to do and be in this world." Why do you think the Church is often reluctant to get out of the pew and get involved in issues like AIDS, poverty or injustice?

4. What do you think the Church is called "to do and be" in this world?

5. Bono has stated, "Any kind of humanitarian work should come first from the Church and should spur along the rest of the world to get involved." What do you think about that thought? What would happen in our world if it were true? What does the Church need to do in order to redeem its place as the leader of humanitarian efforts?

6. What do you think people miss out on when they don't get involved in changing this world and giving themselves away for others?

7. When you think about getting involved in something humanitarian in nature, has God laid anything on your heart? If so, what? (If not, then perhaps the following can become a prayer for your group: *God show us where we can be to proclaim Your love.*)

Going Deeper: Make sure that everyone in the group has an exhaustive concordance for the Scriptures. Before the next group meeting, have each person look up every time Jesus mentions the word "kingdom" in all four Gospels. Make some notes about what you learn about kingdoms from what Jesus says, especially what He says about the "kingdom of God" or the "kingdom of heaven."

CHAPTER 4: HOPE AMIDST DESPAIR

1. The opening quote from this chapter is from a Franciscan Benediction. The entire benediction reads as follows:

   May God bless you with discomfort at easy answers, half truths, and superficial relationships, so that you may live deep within your heart. May God bless you with anger at injustice, oppression, and exploitation of people, so that you may work for injustice, freedom, and peace. May God bless you with tears to shed for those who suffer from pain, rejection, starvation, and war, so that you may reach out your hand to comfort them and to turn their pain into joy. And may God bless you with enough foolishness to believe that you can make a difference in this world, so that you can do what others claim cannot be done. Amen.

   Take a few moments to reflect on this benediction. What phrases connect with you?

2. What did you learn from your research on the orphan crisis in Haiti? What can the Church do?

3. How were you affected by the stories of Thamara, Jabez and Jonas? How did those stories connect with you?

4. Why is it that often the Church gets stuck in the church building? What are some of the reasons why the Church does not venture out "mobilizing its faith"?

5. What are some ways in which your study group can act as Kingdom subjects, proclaiming and embodying the message that the Kingdom has come near?

6. What do you think of the quote, "Be the change you want to see in the world"? What might it look like if we actually lived out that statement?

7. End your group time using the Franciscan Benediction as a prayer of commissioning for your group.

Going Deeper: Now that you've read about what The Hands and Feet Project is trying to do to help the orphan crisis in Haiti, take some time to pray for Drex and Jo, Chris, Mark, Will and the rest as they continue to explore what The Hands and Feet Project should look like in the future. Before the next group meeting, drop Drex and Jo an e-mail through The Hands and Feet Project website at http://www.handsandfeetproject.org. It would be an incredible encouragement to them to know that you're reading this book.

CHAPTER 5: BRINGING HEAVEN HERE

1. In reading the chapter, was there anything that resonated with you? Was there anything that you disagreed with or just didn't get?

2. What did you learn from studying all the times that Jesus mentioned "kingdom" in the four Gospels? What do you think the phrase "the kingdom of God" or "the

kingdom of heaven" meant for Jesus and His listeners?

3. How would you describe the phrase "bringing heaven here" to someone who hasn't read this chapter?

4. What are the implications for how we view and live this life if it's true that the kingdom of God is breaking into this world?

5. "This was what Jesus was inviting people to embrace: A way of living in the present that would go on for all eternity—a way of life that was in harmony with its Creator. A life propelled by compassion, generosity, love and peace." What do you think about that quote? What does it say about the importance of this life? How is this life to be lived?

6. How has this chapter changed your perspective on salvation? On God's plan for the cosmos?

7. What do you think is the role of the followers of Jesus in advancing the Kingdom?

8. What kind of impact should the idea that we are partners with God in bringing heaven to Earth or in advancing the Kingdom have on the way you view this life and those around you?

Going Deeper: Before the next group meeting, each person should do a search on the Internet for the following terms: "Haiti," "orphans," "orphan crisis," "orphanages in Haiti," "children of Haiti," or any other terms regarding the state of orphans in Haiti. What are the needs of the orphans in Haiti? What is currently being done to resolve this orphan crisis? What are people recommending should be done? Can the Church help? If so, how?

CHAPTER 6: GREATER THINGS

1. In this chapter, Chris made the following statement: "Poverty is a moral issue." What do you think that statement means? In what way is poverty a moral issue?

2. Read Mark 6:30-44. What other observations can you make about the story? What implications does the story have for your life?

3. Have you ever been in a situation that you thought was impossible to handle? What has this chapter revealed to you about what is possible with God?

4. This chapter describes the role of a *talmidim*, or disciple, in the first-century Church. Based on this description, are you a true disciple of Christ? Have you committed to making your life look just like His?

5. How can you be the hands and feet of Jesus in your world?

Going Deeper: As a way of closing this chapter of your group's journey, each person should share a little from his or her writings. After each person shares, spend some time praying that his or her life would be reoriented to live more in tune with the kind of life that Jesus is offering and inviting each one to explore.

CHAPTER 7: A LOOK BACK

1. Is there anything that Mark or Will said that connected with you?

2. How were you affected by Tina and Rachel's story? How does that story connect with you?

3. What do you think is the Church's responsibility for people like Rachel and Thamara? How can the Church bring a sense of dignity and humanity to children like these two?

4. Read James 1:27 and Micah 6:8. What new insights have you gained on these passages since reading this book? How has your view changed regarding these verses?

5. What are your thoughts on Mark's illustration about being tied to the dock versus launching out into the open water? How have you seen that to be true in your own life?

6. What are your impressions of the "great descent" that Mark talked about? How does this kind of attitude go against our culture or even against Christian culture?

7. In what ways has this chapter called you to re-examine your life? How will you reorient your life around Jesus' invitation to live the Kingdom kind of life?

Going Deeper: Before the next group meeting, as a way of solidifying the lessons learned along the journey of this book, each person should reflect on the lessons that he or she learned in this book. How has your perspective on God, life, poverty, the Church and the kingdom of God changed? Take a good portion of time and write out some of your thoughts and impressions. Write about the things you have explored and learned and how you want to see your life reoriented around the kind of Kingdom life that Jesus has invited you into. At your last group session, be ready to share a little bit from your writings.

CHAPTER 8: USE YOUR HANDS & FEET

For this last chapter, sit down with your group and talk about how you and those in your small group might team up and get the word out about The Hands and Feet Project. Discuss several creative project ideas as a group.

Going Deeper: As a final activity during the group meeting, hand out paper and pencils and have each group member write an encouraging note to one of The Hands and Feet Project team members. Ask the students to write about what touched them about the story of the Children's Village. When the group members are finished with their letters, put all the letters into a manila envelope and send them to The Hands and Feet Project at the address below.

The Hands and Feet Project
P.O. Box 682105
Franklin, TN 37068-2105

FACTS ABOUT HAITI

Official Name
Haitian Creole: *Repiblik d Ayiti*
French: *République d'Haïti*
English: Republic of Haiti

Geography
Area: 10,714 sq. mi. (27,750 sq. km.)
Location: Bounded on the north by the Atlantic Ocean, on
     the east by the Dominican Republic, on the south by
     the Caribbean Sea, and on the west by the Windward
     Passage.
Capital: Port-au-Prince (18° 32′ N 72°20′ W)
Terrain: Rugged mountains with small coastal plains and
river valleys.
Highest Point: Chaine de la Selle at 8,793 ft. (2,680 m.)
Climate: Warm and semiarid, with high humidity in coastal
     areas. Temperatures in the winter months range from
     55° to 80° F (15° to 25° C) and in the summer months
     from 75° to 95° F (25° to 35° C).
Rainfall: 55 to 80 inches (140 to 200 cm). Heavier rainfall
     occurs on the southern peninsula and in the north-
     ern plains and mountains.
Flora: In 1925, Haiti was a lush tropical paradise, with more
     than 60 percent of its land mass covered with forests.
     Today, only 2 percent of the land is forested (primarily
     consisting of pine forests at high elevations and man-
     groves in inaccessible swamps).

Population

Total Population: 8,308,504 (2006 estimate)
- 0 to 14 years: 42.7 percent (1,770,523 male; 1,749,853 female)
- 15-64 years: 54.2 percent (2,201,957 male; 2,301,886 female)
- 65 years and over: 3.4 percent (125,298 male; 158,987 female)

Largest Cities:
- Port-au-Prince: population 2,000,000
- Cap Haïtien: population 600,000
- Carrefour: population 300,000

Population Growth Rate: 2.3 percent (2006 estimate)

Population Density: 758 people per sq. mi. (293 per sq. km) concentrated mostly in urban areas, coastal plains and valleys.

People

Median Age: 18.2 years (2006 estimate)
- Male: 17.8 years
- Female: 18.6 years

Infant Mortality Rate: 71.65 deaths/1,000 live births (2006 estimate)
- Male: 78.01 deaths/1,000 live births
- Female: 65.1 deaths/1,000 live births

Life Expectancy: 52.23 years (2006 estimate)
- Male: 51.89 years
- Female: 54.6 years

Ethnic Groups:
- Black: 95 percent
- Mulatto and white: 5 percent

Religion: (Note that roughly half of the population also practices vodou)
- Roman Catholic: 80 percent
- Protestant: 16 percent (Baptist: 10 percent; Pentecostal: 4 percent; Adventist: 1 percent; other: 1 percent)
- None: 1 percent
- Other: 3 percent

Literacy Rate: 52.9 percent (2003 estimate)
- Male: 54.8 percent
- Female: 51.2 percent

Official Languages: French and Haitian Creole. Only 10 percent of the population speaks French; many also speak English and Spanish.

Government

Form of Government: Republic

Date of Independence: January 1, 1804

Branches of Government:
- Executive: President
- Legislative: Senate (30 seats); Chamber of Deputies (99 seats)
- Judicial: Court of Cassation

Political Parties and Coalitions: Fanmi Lavalas, Struggling People's Organization, Open the Gate Party, Christian

Movement for a New Haiti, Tet Ansam, Fusion Socialist Democrats, Grand Center Right Front Coalition, Assembly of Progressive National Democrats, Union to Save Haiti, Mobilization for Haiti's Progress, Haitian Democratic and Reform Movement

Eligibility to Vote: Universal at age 18

Economy

Gross Domestic Product: $3.7 billion (2005). Haiti is the least-developed country in the Western Hemisphere and one of the poorest in the world. Haiti ranks 153rd out of the 177 countries in the United Nations' Human Development Index. About 80 percent of the population lives in abject poverty (second to last in the world).

Per Capita Gross Domestic Product: $440 (2005).

Income Sources: Nearly 70 percent of Haitians depend on the agriculture sector, which consists mainly of small-scale subsistence farming. Other income sources include industry and tourism.

Inflation: 15 percent (2005 estimate). At the time of the departure of President Aristide at the end of 2003, the inflation rate stood at 42.7 percent.

Currency: gourde

Minimum Wage: 70 gourdes per day (approximately $1.70 U.S.)

Natural Resources: bauxite, copper, calcium carbonate, gold, marble

Exports: apparel, mangos, leather and raw hides, seafood

Sources:
1. CIA World Factbook: Haiti. http://www.cia.gov/cia/publications/factbook/geos/ha.html.
2. U.S. Department of State Bureau of Western Hemisphere Affairs, "Background Notes on Haiti," March 2006. http://www.state.gov/r/pa/ei/bgn/1982.htm.
3. Wikipedia.com, "Haiti: Geography, Economy, Demographics, Culture." http://en.wikipedia.org/Haiti.
4. World Factbook, "Information on Haiti, Its Geography and History." http://mapsoftheworld.com/country-profile/Haiti.html.

SHORT-TERM MISSIONS
TRIP PLANNER

Now that you've read about the adventures of Mark Stuart and Audio Adrenaline in Haiti, maybe you're thinking about planning a short-term missions trip of your own. Perhaps you're already planning to go on a trip with your own youth or college group, or maybe you're just interested in helping people or in sharing the gospel around the world. If any of these apply, read on. If you have not yet found a trip to go on or a group to go with, please refer to resource pages at the end of this book, where you will find contact information for organizations that can help you arrange to go on your own short-term missions trip to help people around the world.

Of course, before you go, you better be prepared! The first thing to remember is that while you're going to help others, whether by caring for children, building a church, serving food, or sharing the gospel, you are also a guest in another country. You will be going to help others, but it's important to try to understand and be mindful of the new culture that you will find in the foreign country you will be visiting. Be open to learning from the people you meet. Don't view the trip as simply you going to help "the needy," but instead, view the trip as a chance to come alongside people and work toward a common goal.

The following are a few tips to consider as you prepare, followed by a checklist that you can complete prior to leaving for your trip.

TRIP TIPS

Pray. Begin your planning simply, with prayer. Pray about the place you are going to and about the project or the specific role you will play in carrying out your team's goals. If you are going alone with a group such as Youth With A Mission (YWAM) or meeting up with a team of people you don't know, pray for that team of people. If you are going with a local youth group, pray for those friends and acquaintances who are going with you. Pray also for your team's safe travel and health. Pray about all the people you will meet while you are away, that you will make friends, that you will have the opportunity to serve the people you meet, and that you will be able to share your heart with the people God puts in your path. If you have a few weeks left until the trip, try to set aside some time each day to stop and think about the trip, the people, the place you're going, and your purpose there. Lift up these things to God in prayer each day until you leave.

Get Your Passport. If you are going out of the country, process your passport information and photograph far enough in advance so that you can go on the trip. If you arrange to get an expedited passport, you can obtain it in as little as two weeks; otherwise, obtaining a passport will take much longer. Also, while short-term trips to Mexico or Canada at one time did not require you to get a passport, beginning December 31, 2006, all air and sea travelers between the United States, Canada and Mexico will require you to show a passport. From December 31, 2007, all land travelers between these three countries will be required to show a passport.

Research Your Destination. If you have time, do some research on the country or region that you are going to visit with your missions team. If your team hasn't done this, take some time to learn about the land, the people, the culture, the population and even some of the history of the region you will visit. If you can, create a short list of things to remind you of the country or region so that you can be praying for the people each day and be reminded of them specifically.

Prepare Your Body. If you're going to a country overseas, your team leader or youth pastor will most likely provide you with a list of health concerns. Sometimes, you will need to get certain immunizations for specific countries. If this is the case, make sure that you visit your doctor and tell him or her about your trip. Then schedule an appointment to get whatever vaccinations are required. Remember, it is always smart to consult with your doctor before any international trip, whether your team leader recommends it or not.

Pack Your Luggage Well, but Not Too Well. When you pack your luggage, do not seal anything, as security agents will likely search your bags thoroughly (see the checklist for other suggestions).

Fill Out Paper Work. Before you leave, you will need to complete any paperwork given to you by your team leader, including all parental consent forms (if you're under 18) and insurance forms for the group or organization with which you're traveling.

Raise Funds and Support. There are many ways to raise funds for your short-term missions trip. The first (and usually most effective) way to gain support is to write an engaging letter that describes in detail your passion for the people in the foreign country you're visiting and what you hope to accomplish while you're gone. End the letter with a sincere request for prayer and financial support. Send a copy of this letter to friends, family and members of your local church, and then watch how people respond. Remember also to give your supporters a *deadline* for their financial contribution.

SHORT-TERM MISSIONS TRIP CHECKLIST

Bring:

☐ *One* suitcase, larger bag or backpack with your smaller items and books stowed in *one* carry-on. The lighter you can travel, the easier it will be for you to get around. Remember to label each item of your luggage with your name and address, just in case it gets lost.

☐ At least two sets of clothes. Depending on what you will be doing on the trip, make sure your clothes are loose fitting, sturdy and comfortable. Also make sure that your clothes fit well, as you will probably be wearing them again and again.

☐ Work clothes and accessories, especially if you're planning to do any building, construction or other kind of hard work. This includes gloves, hats (for shade), durable pants or shorts and a shirt that you don't mind getting dirty.

☐ One pair of durable shoes. If you are traveling to a worksite, your shoes may get dirty or wet. Be sure that they are comfortable, as you may be wearing them for the duration of the trip.

☐ Sunscreen, especially if you're visiting a country located in a hot climate.

☐ A pillow, depending on your accommodations.

☐ Toiletries, including soap, shampoo, conditioner, toothbrush, toothpaste, chapstick, a razor and shaving gel, toilet paper, deodorant, contact lenses and solution (if you wear them), and aspirin or other over-the-counter medicines you might need. Pack anything that could potentially leak in a clear sealable bag.

☐ Any necessary prescription medicines in their original packaging.

☐ Towel(s) for bathing or swimming.

☐ A book to read.

☐ A pen or pencil for studying, doing devotions or other practical uses.

☐ A camera and film (or batteries, if it is a digital camera).

☐ A list of emergency phone numbers and a copy of your trip itinerary (leave a copy of your itinerary with family or close friends).

☐ Your plane, bus or other transportation tickets.

☐ Any money you intend to bring on the trip for meals or other expenses.

☐ Your Bible. If you have extra room, you might even consider packing several Bibles so that you can leave one or two behind in the foreign land you will be visiting. Some foreign countries have a hard time getting access to Bibles, so this might be a nice gift for someone you will meet.

☐ If you are going to cross an international border during the course of your trip, make sure you have your passport in a handy, safe place inside your carry-on luggage.

☐ Check and recheck that you have everything.

TIPS FOR LEADERS

For new youth leaders or volunteer leaders, planning a short-term missions trip can be a daunting task unless you break down your trip planning into smaller goals. To keep it simple, you will want to determine the following three things first:

1. *Where are you going to go?* This might seem obvious and simplistic, but it will help to do your homework. Does your church have relationships overseas or in bordering countries? Are you aware of any ministries in other countries whose mission resonates strongly with the mission of your church or youth group? Do you have any foreign language speakers in your

church or youth group? Do you have any leaders in your church who have been overseas on a mission trip lately? It is very important that both you and your team have a passion for the people living in the country in which you will serve.

2. *How are you going to help the people in that place?* Assess the needs of the church, organization or ministry you want to help. You might want to partner with a missions-savvy organization to help smooth the way. If you're going independently, you probably want to start by asking the leaders in this mission field exactly how your group could be of help. This is key! You don't want to bring 30 students to a foreign place to be housed and fed for a week if they're not truly needed.

3. *Now ask yourself, why?* "Why?" is truly the biggest question involved in taking your group on a short-term missions trip. Why are you going to this particular location? What do you hope to achieve during the trip? How is God leading you and your group to serve the people you will meet? How will going on this trip meet your hopes and passions biblically? To answer this question is to give your trip a definitive purpose

so that your students and volunteers walk away from the trip changed, knowing that they were effective in their ministry efforts. You might even want to create a teaching series around the focus of the trip to be done before, during or after the trip to help students dive into a particular theme such as service, justice or evangelism.

TRIP-PLANNING SUGGESTIONS

Prepare your team. Prepare your team by doing a series of three to six pre-trip study sessions. During these sessions, share some of the scriptural reasons for going on the trip, the goals of the trip that are shaping your team's expectations and perceptions, and your heart for the place and the people you are going to serve. Talk about and brainstorm ways that each member of the team can contribute to the trip goals. Build some team-building exercises into these prep sessions to help your team develop a bond prior to being in a foreign place together. If any training is required, also prepare one to three training meetings to talk about specific tasks that will be required on the trip, such as construction, teaching, activities or VBS crafts.

Create an Agenda. While you're on the trip, try to create a balanced agenda that will allow your team some free time. Intentionally look for some fun activities that your group can take part in.

Pray. Gather your team to pray before and after each meeting. As the leader of the trip, it is also important to make prayer a regular part of your personal schedule. In addition, recruit a team of intercessors who will pray for you and your team daily while you're away.

Plan a Debriefing Meeting. Schedule at least one debriefing meeting after the trip to share stories and reports and allow your team members to process coming home to America together. Depending on the length of your trip, returning home can be a shock. It is important to praise God for the breakthroughs that happened on the trip, in the people you met, and in the lives and hearts of your team members.

Schedule a Presentation Recapping the Trip. Think about doing a short reception and presentation for the people who supported your trip both financially and in prayer. You could do this in someone's home or at your church. You might even want to ask to give a short presentation in a church service to let the entire congregation know where you went, what you did, and the impact it had on the people you visited and on the team members themselves.

ORGANIZATION
RESOURCE LIST

HANDS & FEET

The following organizations can help you to plan or prepare your own short-term missions trip, whether you are traveling alone or with a team of people.

CRM (Church Resource Ministries)
1240 N. Lakeview Avenue, Suite 120
Anaheim, CA 92807
(800) 777-6658 or (714) 779-0370
www.crmnet.org

Christian Associates International
1534 N. Moorpark Rd. #356
Thousand Oaks, CA 91360
(818) 865-1816
E-mail:
usoffice@christianassociates.org

The Hands and Feet Project
P.O. Box 682105
Franklin, TN 37068-2105
(615) 300-7497
www.hafproject.org

Youth for Christ
P.O. Box 4478
Englewood, CO 80155
(303) 843-9000
E-mail: info@yfc.net
www.yfc.net

Youth With A Mission (YWAM)
P.O. Box 350
Kealakekua, HI 96750
(808) 323-8009
www.ywam.org

Yugo Ministries
P.O. Box 25
San Dimas, CA 91773-0025
(909) 592-6621
E-mail: outreach@yugo.org
www.yugo.org

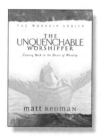

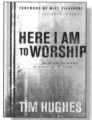

More Breakthrough Books from Soul Sister and Soul Survivor

Connect
The Lowdown on Relationships
and Friendships
Kendall Payne
ISBN 08307.37316

Shine
Beautiful Inside and Out
Aly Hawkins
ISBN 08307.37308

Respect
How to Get It, How to Give It
Jessie Minassian
ISBN 08307.37995

Soul Survivor
Finding Passion and Purpose
in the Dry Places
Mike Pilavachi
ISBN 08307.33248

Trust
Surrendering to God and the
Importance of Forgiveness
Tammy Vervoorn
ISBN 08307.42964

Soul Sister
The Truth About Being
God's Girl
Beth Redman
ISBN 08307.32128

Available at Bookstores Everywhere!

Visit **www.regalbooks.com** to join **Regal's FREE e-newsletter.**
You'll get useful **excerpts from our newest releases** and **special
access to online chats with your favorite authors.** Sign up today!

Regal
God's Word for Your World™
www.regalbooks.com